READER'S DIGEST
**all-season guide
to gardening**

year-round
indoor gardening

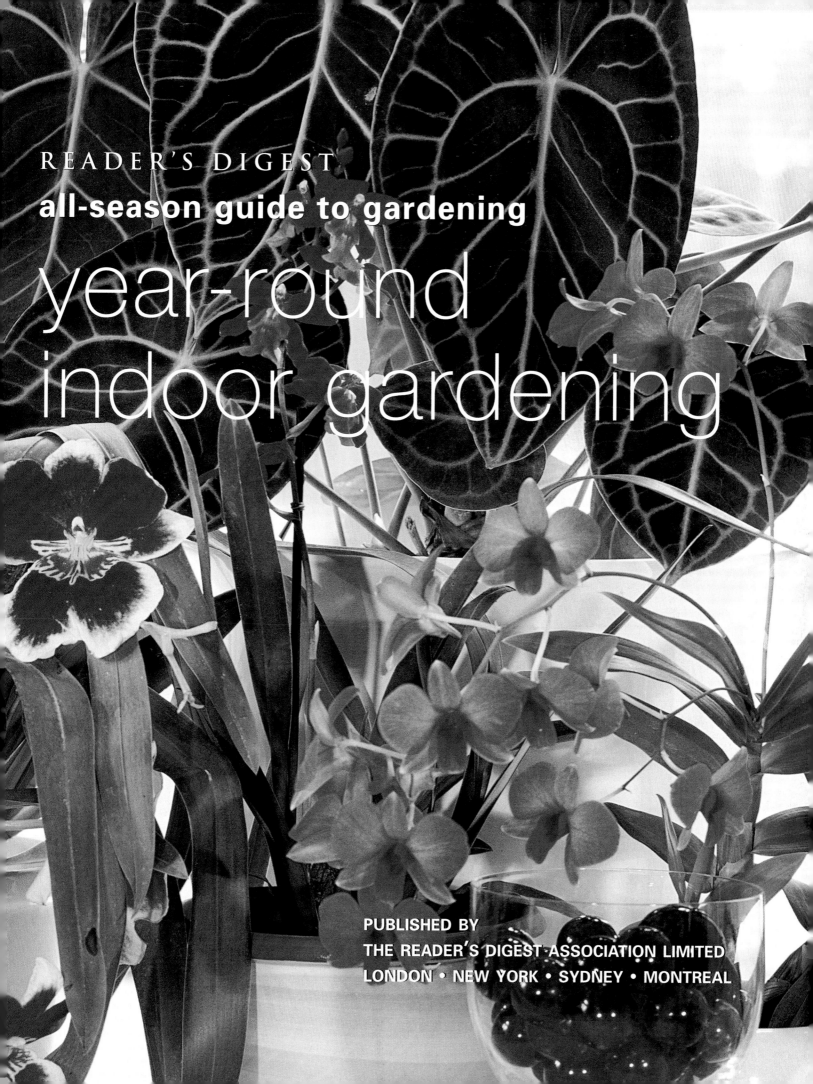

READER'S DIGEST

all-season guide to gardening

year-round
indoor gardening

PUBLISHED BY
THE READER'S DIGEST ASSOCIATION LIMITED
LONDON • NEW YORK • SYDNEY • MONTREAL

contents

about this book

Plants that are grown indoors are commonly referred to as 'houseplants', even though all houseplant species originally come from wild, open-air habitats. Most popular indoor plants are native to tropical or sub-tropical areas of the world: peperomias and begonias from Africa, for example; cacti and fuchsias from central and southern America; hibiscus and ficus from India; spathiphyllum and pandanus from Malaysia; and leptospermum and callistemon from Australia.

The indoor care of such tender rarities used to be a novel way of gardening, but is now an accepted part of interior design and everyday living. For anyone without a garden, it is also the only way to grow hardy species and edible crops, as well as the more familiar exotic houseplants.

Since the indoor environment is comparatively constant, many plants stay in good condition all year round. Changing light levels and day lengths, however, together with natural growth cycles, mean that the majority of houseplants have quite distinct active and resting periods. It is important, therefore, to understand how to care for your plant's needs around the year. Most houseplants fail because they have too much or too little of some vital growth factor such as light, humidity or ventilation. Fortunately, giving them individual care is often easier than tending plants in the garden, because indoor specimens are close at hand and you become more familiar with their needs and behaviour. In return they can give you a lot of pleasure. It is no coincidence that, given the choice, most people tend to sit where they can see plants.

Houseplants are superb styling accessories and can make a huge contribution to a particular decor. Palms, gloxinias (*Sinningia*) and aspidistras are distinctly Victorian in look,

plant names explained

The way that plants are named follows a logical pattern that is based on an international system in use since the 18th century. Names are written according to botanical conventions using a hierarchical system of classification.

- The **genus name** is given first and appears in italics, for example, *Stromanthe* or *Cordyline*. After the first use in an article, and until another genus is mentioned, this is abbreviated to only the initial letter (for example, *S.* or *C.*) for additional plant suggestions within the same genus.

- The genus name is generally followed by the **species name** and this, too, appears in italics. For example, in *Stromanthe sanguinea* (plant 1, below), *sanguinea* is the species name. The species name can be abbreviated to 'sp.' in plant lists.

- When species show **minor variations** in character, they are given a third italicised name, prefixed by 'subsp.' (subspecies), 'var.' (varietas) or 'f.' (forma) in roman letters. For example, *Ceropegia linearis* subsp. *woodii*, *Codiaeum variegatum* var. *pictum* and *Acer palmatum* f. *atropurpureum*.

while orchids have a country-house feel, and spiky cordylines or strelitzias suit the contemporary industrial look.

In addition to their aesthetic value, houseplants possess various other beneficial properties: during the day their leaves diffuse oxygen into the air and absorb carbon dioxide, so indoor plants can be good for your health. Of particular note are lilies and spathiphyllums, said to reduce stress and headaches; air-cleansing spider plants (*Chlorophytum*) and rubber plants (*Ficus elastica*); and begonias and scindapsus, which are some of the most efficient plants for boosting oxygen levels.

All these and many more houseplants are to be found in this volume of the *All-Season Guide to Gardening* series. The book is divided into four key sections:

inspirations offers design ideas and combinations of plants in different seasons. It also suggests some indoor plants whose foliage characteristics make them great all-year plants, or particularly suited to certain locations and lighting levels.

houseplant care is a comprehensive guide to the conditions indoor plants prefer and the best ways to supply these. Day-to-day care is explained in depth, together with more periodic attention, such as repotting, pruning and propagation. Specialised techniques such as forcing plants and cultivation in water (hydroculture) are also covered.

plant selector is an extensive directory of more than 100 houseplants, arranged alphabetically by botanical name or plant type. All the most popular indoor plants are covered, with specific information on their care and maintenance, as well as plants that are suitable for growing alongside them.

more plant ideas offers creative suggestions for ways to display plants in attractive and appropriate containers, including bottle gardens and terrariums. Specialist plant groups such as orchids, cacti and bonsai have their own pages, as do plants that can fill your house with fragrances.

- An artifically bred plant is known as a **cultivated variety** (abbreviated to 'cultivar' or 'cv.'). The cultivar name appears in roman letters, for example, *Cordyline australis* 'Torbay Dazzler' (plant 8, below) and *Impatiens* New Guinea Group (plant 3, below).
- A **hybrid** is a cross between two different plants. Hybrids are indicated by a multiplication sign, for example, *Begonia* x *corallina* and x *Fatshedera lizei*.
- Where a plant has a vernacular or **common name**, this is given before the botanical name, for example, cape primrose (*Streptocarpus*) (plant 2, below) and venus fly trap (*Dionaea muscipula*) (plant 4, below).

key to plants shown below

1 *Stromanthe sanguinea*
2 *Streptocarpus* cv.
3 *Impatiens* New Guinea Group
4 *Dionaea muscipula*
5 *Pachystachys lutea*
6 *Echinocactus* sp., *Mammillaria* sp.
7 *Capsicum annuum* cv.
8 *Cordyline australis* 'Torbay Dazzler'

The mainstay of houseplant displays are the foliage plants, with their wonderful variety of multicoloured and green leaves. However, plant lovers soon discover that growing plants indoors is also a rewarding way to reflect the seasons. Temporary plants, such as spring bulbs, can brighten interiors for up to several months. Miniature roses and annuals, for example cornflowers, bloom in summer, chrysanthemums cheer up autumn, and poinsettias are now traditional at Christmas. Long-term houseplants have their flowering and fruiting seasons, too: the kaffir lily (Clivia miniata) starts to bloom in March, cyclamen flowers in autumn, and winter cherry (Solanum), as its common name implies, does its bit in winter.

inspirations

Anthurium andraeanum cultivar

signs of spring

The fresh, vibrant colours of early flowering plants – such as bulbs, or camellias and primroses – bring the promise of spring right into your home. Enhance their effect by choosing a variety of pots.

Potted camellias (above left) can be brought indoors, where their flowers will be unmarked by frost, rain and wind. Their showy blooms will brighten a cool but well-lit spot. When they have finished flowering, put them back outdoors.

Low-growing tulips, bought in bud, are arranged here with two-toned primroses (*Primula vulgaris*) to create an unmissable splash of colour (left). The individual plant pots can simply be placed in the outer container, or plant them in the outer pot on a layer of pebbles, for drainage.

Cheerful daffodils never fail to raise the spirits (above). These *Narcissus* 'Tête-à-tête' are arranged in complementary containers for single bulbs and groups. Display the plants in a bright yet cool position.

The pretty blue blooms of grape hyacinth (*Muscari*) will brighten any room (above). They can be found in small pots in practically every garden centre in early spring. These ones have been put into basket-work containers and finished off with a top-dressing of moss on the compost.

When the kaffir lily (*Clivia miniata*) sends up its flowering stems, that is the signal to start watering the plant freely. It will then produce these impressive orange flowers (below). For the rest of the year, it should be watered only sparingly.

Crocus and *Iris reticulata* (above right, from right to left) can be 'forced' to produce their flowers earlier than usual. During autumn, simply plant the corms or bulbs in bulb fibre, in pots with drainage holes. Stand the pots outside until the shoots develop, then bring them indoors to flower.

The easter cactus (*Hatiora gaertneri*) hails from the forests of Brazil, which explains the plant's liking for high humidity. For a dramatic display of exotic pink flowers, use cactus compost and keep the plant in bright filtered light.

summer blooms

Indoor plants make their strongest growth during summer and many will be at their peak now. For a perfect complement to their lush foliage – or to replace indoor plants enjoying a temporary break outside – try introducing pot plants with lively flowers.

Cornflowers (*Centaurea cyanus*) (left) and other potted annuals bought in bud will remain in flower considerably longer than a bunch of cut flowers, and they are cheap to replace. This is one of the best ways of enjoying the essence of a cottage garden within the confines of a house.

Pots of miniature roses are hard to resist. Here (right) they are matched with icelandic poppies (*Papaver croceum*). Either discard the roses after flowering or trim them by two-thirds, repot into a larger container and place outside. Bring them back indoors when flower buds reappear.

Repetition is invaluable as a display tool indoors as well as out: these matching slipper flowers (*Calceolaria* Herbeohybrida Group) benefit from being in identical containers (below). Kept in medium light, the plants should bloom through late spring and summer. In the background two maidenhair ferns (*Adiantum raddianum*) – also in matching containers – add year-round interest.

The bell-shaped, purple flowers of *Campanula carpatica* create a summery mound (above), which looks marvellous in a small area where space is at a premium. Pretty bowls make ideal drip trays for houseplants, but line them first with polythene to protect the surface from water marks.

There are many cultivars of *Hibiscus rosa-sinensis* (above right). Their tropical-looking blooms have prominent stamens and the dark glossy foliage is a perfect foil for the large, colourful flowers. These plants like good but indirect light.

A series of contemporary containers unifies this group of plants (above) and displays them at varying heights. Kalanchoe, gold and silver-leaved *Soleirolia soleirolii*, *Sansevieria trifasciata* 'Laurentii' and daisy-flowered *Gerbera jamesonii* provide an eye-catching range of shapes, colours and textures.

As climbers, the hoop-trained ivy (*Hedera*) and purple-flowered passion flower (*Passiflora*) add height to this simple but effective plant grouping (right). The display is completed by hardy *Geranium* x *magnificum*, which flowers in profusion in summer. All three plants thrive best in a bright position.

autumn hues

As light intensities start to fade in autumn, light-loving houseplants should be moved to brighter spots, near a window. Central heating will dry the air, so regularly mist plants with a fine spray once the heating is on.

Many cultivars of coloured-leaved crotons (*Codiaeum variegatum*) carry the warm yellows, reds, purples and russets of autumn (left). These evergreen houseplants can last for years: stable, warm temperatures and high levels of humidity help to keep them healthy.

Cheerful potted chrysanthemums (right) last longer than cut flowers, and there are masses of different colours to choose from. Look for ones with healthy foliage and a mixture of opened flowers and fat buds. Potted chrysanthemums can be planted in the garden after they have finished flowering, although they usually lose their dwarf habit.

Bead plant (*Nertera granadensis*) has a coat of striking orange berries that will last right through autumn and winter. These low-growing plants form a mound about 5cm (2in) high.

In autumn, the shops are full of tempting, pepper-scented cyclamen, their buds like furled umbrellas opening to jewel-coloured flowers (above). They love a cool, bright spot and will flower throughout winter. Plants can be kept for years – some indoor gardeners have tubers 40 years old.

The ornamental winter cherry (*Solanum pseudocapsicum*) bears its decorative, inedible fruit for several months during autumn and winter (right). Stand the plant outdoors in summer and it will flower and set fruit again.

An indoor garden in unusual containers is fun to create using a mixture of exotic plants (below). Cacti and flamingo flower (*Anthurium scherzerianum*), with its red, waxy spathes, and bead plant in the bottom left corner, are some of the weird and wonderful plants in this eye-catching group of houseplants.

This showy bromeliad, *Tillandsia cyanea* (right), is from Ecuador. The pink, paddle-shaped structures are its bracts, from which develop a succession of purple flowers. Tillandsia loves warm, moist air so should be mist-sprayed.

winter cheer

Since ancient times, people have brought plants inside during winter to help raise spirits when days are short and the weather cold. Lively foliage, flowers and fruits are especially welcome, and provide a contrast to the sleeping garden outside.

Spring can seem just around the corner when common snowdrops (*Galanthus nivalis*) are in bloom (above). Here, a few small pots of these early bulbs are simply set in a basket painted pale green. They will last best in a cool place, away from radiators and fires.

Winter-flowering narcissi are easy to force into bloom (right). Either leave the potted bulbs outside, covered and protected by a thick layer of compost, until they start to develop shoots, or stand them in a cool, dark, frost-free place indoors. When the flower buds show, bring them indoors; tie their stems if necessary to stop them toppling over.

The pretty calamondin orange (x *Citrofortunella microcarpa*) is petite enough to make an ideal indoor plant (left). It is rarely without fragrant white blossom or fruit. Good winter light, soft water and a citrus fertiliser keep plants in good health. They like to be moved outdoors for the summer.

Cymbidium orchids (above left) send up long flower spikes throughout autumn and winter. The fat buds open into stately, exotic and long-lasting flowers.

For potfuls of colour, *Begonia* Elatior hybrids are hard to beat (above centre) and there are plenty of hues to choose from. They last well, provided they are positioned in bright but indirect light.

Amaryllis (*Hippeastrum*) are spectacular flowering houseplants (above right), and surprisingly easy to grow. Within a few weeks of planting the bulb, a flower bud will appear, followed by the leaves.

Florists' cinerarias (right), now known as pericallis, are a showy mass of daisy-like flowers. These are grown as annuals, so enjoy them while they are looking good, then discard them with a clear conscience.

The colourful bracts of poinsettias (below) look especially appropriate during the festive season. It is best to let light and air reach all the leaves and stems, so do not place the plant in a very deep container.

year-round greens

It is generally believed that plants improve the air quality inside buildings, and the soothing greens of indoor foliage plants are good for our well-being, too. Choose leafy plants for their shapes and textures, then see what a calming effect they have.

There are many cultivars of peace lily (*Spathiphyllum*), ranging in height from 20cm (8in) to 1.2m (4ft). If kept in bright indirect light, the mass of green leaves may be supplemented by white, sail-like flower structures in spring and summer (left).

The sculptural succulent leaves of *Aloe vera* make a dramatic silhouette (right), while the sap of this popular indoor plant is well-known for its healing properties and as an ingredient in many cosmetic products.

The creeping fig (*Ficus pumila*) has a luxuriant profusion of small, deep green leaves and trails prettily (below). This plant must never be allowed to dry out.

Anthuriums like constant warmth coupled with high levels of humidity (above centre). Under ideal growing conditions, they produce a succession of large leaves and shiny, exotic flower structures of white, red or pink, tinged with green.

The fresh greens of umbrella plant (*Cyperus involucratus*) (above left) are welcome in any room, but these watery sedges seem most at home in the bathroom. Impossible to overwater, the umbrella plant is happiest when permanently standing in water.

The fiddle-leaf fig (*Ficus lyrata*) has huge, shiny, mid-green leaves with contrasting paler undersides (left). This unusual fig likes warm temperatures and prefers to be placed alongside other plants.

Long strands of ivy (*Hedera*) have a dramatic effect when given space to dangle like a green curtain (above). The medium light and cool airy space provided by this staircase create ideal growing conditions for these common but beautiful foliage plants.

Different foliage shapes and shades of green can complement each other (below). Here are *Ficus benjamina* 'Natasja', boston fern (*Nephrolepis exaltata* 'Bostoniensis') and dainty maidenhair fern (*Adiantum raddianum*).

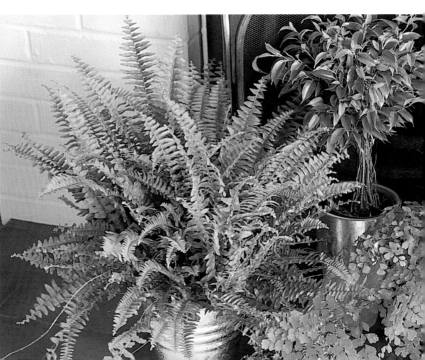

year-round colours

Leaf colours can be as lively and varied as flowers – and last longer. The leaf pigments, or variegation, can create regular patterns, contrasting edgings, or more haphazard spots, stripes and streaks.

The foliage of aptly named *Tradescantia fluminensis* 'Quadricolor' (above) shows almost every permutation of green, cream and pink. Good light brings out the best colours.

Rosary vine (*Ceropegia linearis* subsp. *woodii*) is an easy succulent to grow indoors (left). Its long dangling stems of small, marbled, heart-shaped leaves develop from a woody tuber.

Among the finest indoor specimen houseplants are those in the *Dracaena fragans* Deremensis Group (right). Long-lived and virtually indestructible, these evergreen shrubs from tropical Africa bear a lush profusion of long, handsomely striped leaves.

The light and dark patterns on the leaves of *Dieffenbachia seguine* 'Reflector' (above centre) are typical of this fabulously marked genus. These plants thrive best in company with others, where a warm, humid micro-environment forms around their leaves and stems.

The prayer plant family shows a wide range of foliage colours with a hint of tropical flamboyance. Of Brazilian origin, *Stromanthe sanguinea* 'Triostar' (above right) has striking dark green leaves marked with green and cream and suffused with burgundy underneath. Stand plants on wide saucers of moistened pebbles to raise humidity.

The leaf markings of rex-type begonias are among the most beautiful in the plant world, ably demonstrated by the silver, red and green markings of *Begonia* 'Benitochiba' (above). This rhizomatous group of begonias appreciates moderate levels of light and careful watering, especially in winter when they should be barely moist.

A single polka dot plant (*Hypoestes phyllostachya*) is interesting, but a large group is spectacular and not expensive to achieve, as these plants are cheap to buy (below). Choose from pink dots or splashes on green leaves, and green veining on red, pink or white leaves. Keep the plants compact by pinching out flower spikes.

A variegated ivy (*Hedera*), cordyline, succulent crassula and ivy-leaved pelargonium in a hanging basket stand out in this group of varied indoor foliage plants (right). If you buy several plants at the same time, their foliage colours and shapes can be matched up in the shop, where you can try out different plant groupings.

houseplant care

Owning a collection of houseplants is a bit like being permanently surrounded by friends, and caring for them is incredibly satisfying. To get to know your plants, try to imagine them in their natural habitats – evoking a stony desert, cool mountain forest or steamy tropical jungle can help when it comes to judging a plant's cultural needs. Appropriate levels of light and temperature, as well as careful watering, will ensure a plant's survival, while feeding it and keeping its leaves free of dust and pests will keep it in tiptop condition. It is important to recognise when a plant has grown too large for its pot and needs replanting, and a knowledge of propagation will enable you to raise your own new houseplants.

Misting *Billbergia* and *Tillandsia* species

choosing a plant

Most houseplants will thrive in your home as long as their specific needs are met. To avoid disappointment, select plants for which you can provide a suitable environment, as some plants enjoy a sunny windowsill while others require relatively high humidity or a cool position.

deciding what you want

Before you buy an indoor plant, consider the following:

● **which room?** Temperature and humidity levels vary from one room to another, and a plant that might flourish in a humid bathroom could be unhappy in a cool study.

● **aspect** The direction in which a window faces will affect the amount of light available in a room. Some plants need bright light or even full sun; others prefer indirect light.

● **flowers or foliage?** Decide whether you want attractive foliage all year round, or an eye-catching display of flowers or berries in a particular season. Some plants, especially those with variegated leaves, may combine more than one of these features.

● **size** How much space have you got to accommodate a full-grown plant? Some plants, such as polka dot plant (*Hypoestes phyllostachya*), take up comparatively little room, while others, such as a grape ivy (*Cissus rhombifolia*), rapidly reach 2m (6ft) or more, unless pruned back.

● **cost** Popular houseplants such as spider plants, ivies (*Hedera*) and cyclamen are fairly cheap to buy and easy to replace. A palm or orchid, on the other hand, can be expensive. Before purchasing a costly specimen, consider carefully whether you know how to look after it and can give it the care and the environment it needs.

● **maturity** Expect to pay more for a mature houseplant, and to give it extra special care while it is getting used to its new

An african violet (below) will remain small, so several can be planted together, whereas a vigorous *Ficus longifolia* (right) can reach a house ceiling within a few years.

easy houseplants **to grow**

If you are not yet confident of your growing skills, or want a plant that needs little attention and can tolerate a wide range of conditions, choose from the following:

● *Abutilon* ● african violet (*Saintpaulia*)
● *Aspidistra* ● cacti and succulents (many)
● *Chamaedorea* ● *Chlorophytum* ● *Cissus*
● coleus (*Solenostemon*) ● *Dracaena*
● dumb cane (*Dieffenbachia*) ● x *Fatshedera*
● *Fatsia* ● *Monstera* ● *Pelargonium* (left) ● pick-a-back plant (*Tolmiea*) ● *Sansevieria* ● *Tradescantia*

surroundings. A small plant is often easier to manage, and can last longer before it outgrows its position.

● **special purposes** Plants can improve the atmosphere of the home and office by lifting the spirits and raising the humidity. Gerbera, nephrolepis and certain other plants also have the capacity to 'clean the air' by removing harmful chemical compounds such as carbon monoxide from cigarette smoke or formaldehyde, given off by carpets and foam insulation.

temporary plants

Some flowering houseplants are intended for short-term display and, like cut flowers, are discarded once they are past their best. These include cinerarias (*Pericallis cruentus*), chrysanthemums, *Exacum affine*, greenhouse primulas and bead plants (*Nertera granadensis*). Others such as gerberas and winter cherry (*Solanum pseudocapsicum*) can be kept from one year to the next, although they may need special care during winter or while they are resting. Annuals, such as capsicums, will die after flowering and fruiting.

choosing a variety

Plants within the same genus can vary widely in appearance and growing requirements, so you need to consider the following qualities of a specific plant.

● **habit** Plants may be upright (such as cyperus, *Ficus elastica*, yucca), arching (such as nephrolepis, spathiphyllum,

Begonia makes an excellent houseplant, and there are lots of varieties to choose from with different habits and leaf colours. Here the vivid red leaves of evergreen *B. rex* provide an eye-catching contrast to the delicate maidenhair fern (*Adiantum capillus-veneris*). Tuberous begonias with richly coloured flowers might also go well with this fern.

spider plant), rosetted (such as agave, aloe, echeveria), bushy (such as *Euphorbia milii*, impatiens, justicia, peperomia) or climbing (such as *Hoya carnosa*, jasmine, stephanotis).

● **leaf shape** The huge variation in leaf shape can influence a plant's impact within a room. Plants with large dramatic leaves include monstera, philodendron and howea. At the other extreme are the dainty leaves of asparagus fern (*Asparagus setaceus*), ceropegia and *Ficus pumila*.

● **leaf colour** Foliage may be plain green or patterned with startling colours. Vivid plants, such as crotons (*Codiaeum*), cordylines and coleus (*Solenostemon*), need either to harmonise or contrast with your room décor.

● **flowers** The shape, size and colour of a plant's flowers affects container you choose and its position within the room. For example, bold-flowered hippeastrum needs lots of space and will look good in a simple but striking pot.

patterns of growth

Houseplants look best if they are positioned to suit their size and habit. Large upright specimens are best placed on the floor, while arching ones look good in a hanging basket.

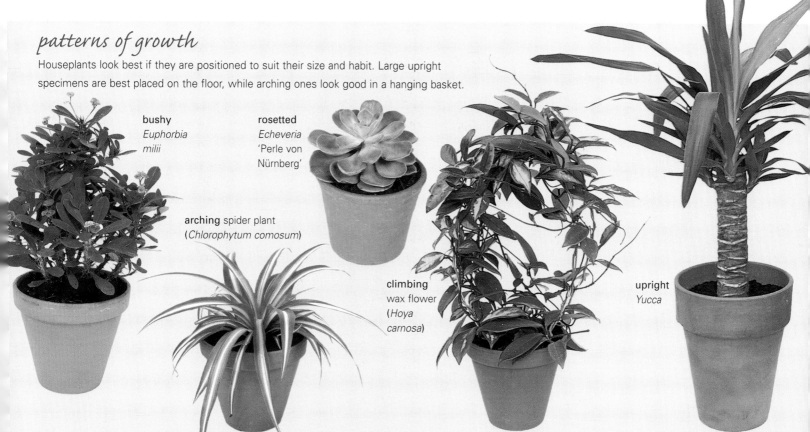

bushy
Euphorbia milii

rosetted
Echeveria 'Perle von Nürnberg'

arching spider plant (*Chlorophytum comosum*)

climbing wax flower (*Hoya carnosa*)

upright *Yucca*

selecting a pot

Choosing the right container will make all the difference to how a plant looks. There are so many styles and sizes, there is bound to be one that complements both the plant and its surroundings. You can either plant directly into a chosen pot, or place an already potted plant into a larger, decorative container.

matching pots to plants

Choose a container to suit a plant's growth habit. Simple containers can flatter delicate or subtle leaf colours and shapes, whereas bold-foliaged plants and many flowering ones may be set off better by a bold or decorative pot. The extremes of a shallow dish or a tall pot can exaggerate the stem lengths on trailing plants.

Containers and plants also need to work within the context of their surroundings. A stark metal pot with a desert cactus or cordyline looks great in a modern interior, but would be out of place in more cluttered Victorian-style surroundings, where, for example, a flamingo flower (*Anthurium andraeanum*) would make a better impact.

pot types

Houseplant containers come in three main types – standard pots, potholders, and larger containers and troughs – plus more specialised containers for plants with special needs.

● **standard pots** are generally made of clay or plastic and have one or more drainage holes in the base. They are sometimes glazed or decorated, and they may be available with a matching saucer or drip tray. Some pots have a built-in drip tray, and others have an internal reservoir beneath a perforated false floor, which can be accessed by water roots. All these pots can be used either freestanding or suspended.

Recycle objects such as aluminium or other metal cans by using them for planting pots, here for herbs such as rosemary, mint, thyme and parsley.

● **potholders** are simply pots or bowls without drainage holes that are used to contain and hide a standard pot. They may be made of almost any material – clay, porcelain, metal, wood, wickerwork or bamboo. Improvised potholders can vary from a teapot or aluminium can (left) to a cane basket.

● **larger containers** and troughs are useful for displaying groups of individually potted plants. They rarely have drainage holes. Other large containers have water reservoirs or a self-watering device.

● **hanging pots and baskets** are suitable for trailing plants such as chlorophytums and goldfish plants (*Columnea*). Types with built-in drip trays are ideal for indoor displays.

● **terrariums** provide a draught-free home for moisture-loving plants such as some delicate ferns, chamaedoreas or prayer plants (*Maranta*) (see page 132).

● **large glass jars and carboys** can be used to make bottle gardens for slow-growing sensitive plants such as calatheas, painted net leaf (*Fittonia*) and pileas (see page 132).

● **pans** and other shallow containers are suitable for dish gardens of small cacti and succulents that do not have deep rooting systems (see page 140).

water drainage

Plants in standard pots with drainage holes need to be placed inside a potholder or on a drip saucer to prevent water from spoiling carpets and furniture, but take care not to leave a plant sitting in drained water for any length of time. Containers without drainage holes or an internal drainage facility need a generous bottom layer of coarse

The material, shape and texture of a plant pot should complement the plant grown in it. Together the plant and pot should form a balanced composition in harmony with the surroundings. *Tillandsia cyanea* (far left) is here planted in a rounded pot, which suits its arching habit, while this stocky, Chinese-style porcelain container balances a profusion of white-flowered primulas (left). The natural habitat of woody-stemmed schleffera (above) is echoed in a brown basketwork outer container.

types of pots

Hanging baskets may have built-in drip trays to hold water.

Some pots have drainage holes and a matching saucer.

Shallow pans should ideally have several drainage holes.

Glazed pots without holes need a drainage layer in the base.

Standard pots and pans, in clay and plastic, come in a wide range of shapes and sizes to suit plants from small seedlings to well-established and mature houseplants.

gravel or crushed polystyrene blocks topped with charcoal, so plants do not become waterlogged. The potting compost can go on top of this drainage layer, or plants in standard pots can be set on it.

positioning plants

The siting of houseplants is crucial to their success and to your enjoyment of them. In addition to the light and temperature needs of the plants (see pages 28 and 30), bear in mind the following points.

● **for your own safety,** keep plants away from electrical appliances and sockets to avoid any risk of electric shocks when watering.

● **stand large specimens** where they cannot be knocked over or bumped into.

● **choose the right-sized pot** for a plant. A small plant in a large pot looks silly, because it is out of proportion, while a tall or very bushy plant in a small plastic pot will appear cramped and is almost certain to be

unstable. For stability, use ceramic pots and heavy soil-based composts for such plants.

● **hang suspended pots or baskets** where people cannot bang their heads on them. Make sure the supports are strong and secure.

● **never stand pots directly** on furniture or any other surface that is easily marked.

● **keep only small plants** on narrow windowsills. A large plant might easily be knocked over, and if the foliage rests against the glass it could be scorched or frosted.

● **extreme or fluctuating temperatures** cause stress to plants, so avoid positions near radiators and open fires. Unless the window is double-glazed, bring windowsill plants inside the curtains on cold winter nights.

● **avoid cold draughts,** which chill the foliage, causing it to curl, turn yellow or develop brown edges before falling prematurely. Fresh air, however, is generally beneficial for most houseplants and stops them developing grey mould and other diseases.

light levels

Sunlight provides plants with the energy to make food, and their physical structure is finely tuned to the amount they receive in their natural surroundings. Too much light can be as detrimental as not enough, so find out about your plants' needs and provide the correct conditions in your home.

natural light

Plants need light when they are actively growing, but not necessarily while dormant or resting. Exactly when and how much light a plant requires depends on its origin and can affect where it is placed in a room. Woodland and forest plants such as dracaenas, cordylines and aspleniums, naturally grow in dappled shade, so can cope with the semi-shade or filtered light of a sunless window, or should be placed about 1.5m (5ft) away from a sunny window. Desert cacti, succulents, pelargoniums and other sun-loving flowering plants revel in the bright light of a sunny windowsill. Most houseplants need something between these two extremes – an east or west-facing window, or bright but not direct sunlight. Very few plants thrive in deep shade – that is, 2m (6ft) or more from a source of natural light.

You can help your houseplants to grow better by taking into account the following points.

● **light levels near windows** fluctuate with the seasons, so consider moving plants closer to

Plants grow towards light, so give their pots a quarter turn clockwise once a week to encourage a well-balanced shape – unlike this lop-sided syngonium (above).

The stromanthe (left) is showing signs of foliage scorch. To prevent this, move plants away from windows at the height of summer, when light levels are very intense.

a window in winter and farther away in summer.
● **most plants lean** towards the main light source. Unless a plant specifically dislikes being turned, occasionally move the pots of your plants clockwise to prevent uneven growth.
● **a mirror can reflect light** into the darker side of the room, and this will benefit plant growth.
● **foliage plants** tolerate low light levels better than flowering ones. Variegated plants need brighter light than green ones to retain their distinctive leaf colouring.

artificial light

Any indoor lighting can enhance forms and colours and add drama to a display of houseplants, but to improve growing conditions requires a special type of light bulb – ordinary tungsten light bulbs are ineffective. Professional growers use mercury or sodium plant lamps. Fluorescent tubes are an effective supplement to natural daylight, but only if they are suspended 60–90cm (2–3ft) above the foliage.

To make a real difference you need 1000 lux, that is about 120 watts, per square metre (yard), which would require four 32-watt fluorescent tubes or a single 125-watt high-pressure mercury bulb.

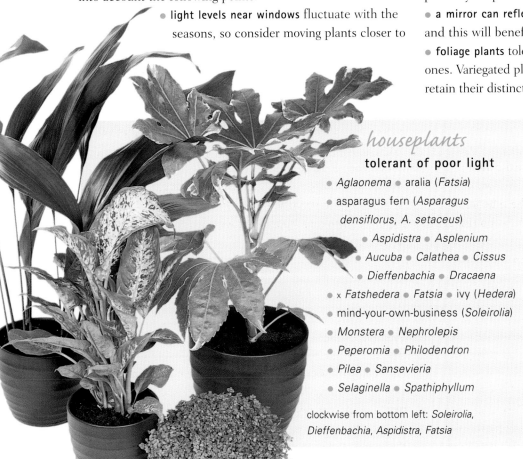

houseplants
tolerant of poor light

● Aglaonema ● aralia (*Fatsia*)
● asparagus fern (*Asparagus densiflorus, A. setaceus*)
● Aspidistra ● Asplenium
● Aucuba ● Calathea ● Cissus
● Dieffenbachia ● Dracaena
● x Fatshedera ● Fatsia ● ivy (*Hedera*)
● mind-your-own-business (*Soleirolia*)
● Monstera ● Nephrolepis
● Peperomia ● Philodendron
● Pilea ● Sansevieria
● Selaginella ● Spathiphyllum

clockwise from bottom left: *Soleirolia, Dieffenbachia, Aspidistra, Fatsia*

Some bromeliads, such as this flaming sword (*Vriesea splendens*), like bright direct light and also tolerate dry air. They thrive on a sunny windowsill in a centrally heated house and produce long-lasting flowers.

some houseplants
that enjoy summer outside

- *Abutilon* ● aralia (*Fatsia*)
- *Aspidistra* ● cacti
- *Chlorophytum* ● Christmas cactus (*Schlumbergera*)
- *Cissus* ● dwarf pomegranate (*Punica granatum* var. *nana*)
- *Epiphyllum* ● jasmine (*Jasminum*) ● mind-your-own-business (*Soleirolia*) ● *Nephrolepis*
- passion flower (*Passiflora*)

summer care

Even though light levels are at their highest in the house during summer, many houseplants appreciate a period outdoors, where gentle rain can refresh their foliage, and light and humidity levels are often higher. The time to move them out is around the longest day, once there is no risk of frosts, and strong gales are unlikely. Houseplants can stay outdoors until the nights draw in and begin to cool down in late summer.

Plants that benefit from an outdoor holiday include evergreens with shiny leaves, such as citrus and dwarf pomegranates, and forest cacti such as Christmas cactus and epiphyllums. Shade-loving species such as aspidistras that enjoy cool or moderate temperatures can also enjoy the summer outside. Never move out plants with furry leaves, such as african violet (*Saintpaulia*) and some begonia species. Tender plants, such as anthuriums and prayer plants (*Maranta*), that need high summer temperatures must be kept indoors or transferred to a warm, shaded greenhouse where they are safe from wind and bright sunlight.

If you live in a flat or have no suitable garden, your plants can still benefit from extra summer light and ventilation through an open window or door. Pelargoniums, busy lizzies (*Impatiens*) and most succulents will enjoy this so long as they are not in a draught.

suitable outdoor positions

Most houseplants that enjoy summer outside need a sheltered place where they are shielded from wind and scorching sunlight. The shady side of a house or wall, or near a hedge (not under trees, though, because drips can damage their foliage) is ideal, or you can stand them in a shaded coldframe with the lid removed. Check them daily because their compost can dry out very quickly. To save on watering, you can plunge pots into the ground or into larger containers filled with sand or shingle.

temperature

Houseplants come from a wide range of environmental conditions, from cool shady forests to hot sunny deserts. Most benefit from seasonal changes in their ambient temperature, depending on whether they are in full growth or temporarily resting.

Every plant has an optimum temperature range within which it grows well. Aim for steady warmth – close to the top of the preferred range – during the plant's growing season, and nearer the bottom level while it is resting, or dormant. Although plants dislike great fluctuations in temperature, which can cause their leaves to turn yellow quickly and drop, most plants are fairly adaptable and will frequently adjust to slightly cooler or warmer conditions. In general, the difference between day and night-time temperatures should be no more than 5°C (10°F).

The majority of houseplants come from tropical and sub-tropical areas, but few thrive indoors in very warm conditions because the atmosphere is too dry – high temperatures in the natural habitat would usually be matched by high levels of light and humidity. If the temperature is not to their liking, plants can show signs of distress:

- **too warm** – thin spindly growth, especially in poor light; leaves turn brown at the edges; flowers fade prematurely.
- **too cold** – leaves curl and turn brown; growth is slow; compost stays wet, causing roots to rot.

rest periods

As temperatures fall in autumn and the hours of daylight continue to decrease, the rate of photosynthesis needed for growth slows down and many plants enter their annual resting period, or dormancy.

Some bulbs and tuberous plants, such as gloxinias and gloriosas, lose their foliage and become fully dormant. They can be moved and kept almost completely dry in temperatures about 5°C (10°F) cooler than in summer.

The growth of other houseplants, especially evergreens, merely slows down in winter. Give these plants less water than in summer, and it is sometimes beneficial to provide cooler conditions elsewhere in the house, but don't let the compost

When a resting plant shows signs of life by producing a leaf or flower bud, like this cyclamen, watering should recommence.

houseplant temperature guide

7°C (45°F)
The minimum for hardy plants, such as *Cyclamen persicum*, and those resting in winter.

10–15°C (50–60°F)
The best range for desert cacti (here a mammillaria), evergreens and most flowering plants.

15°C (60°F)
The minimum for most tender plants, including *Aechmea fasciata*.

15–21°C (60–70°F)
The best range for palms, such as *Howea fosteriana*, and for forest cacti and succulents.

dry out completely. Check each plant about once a week for dead or discoloured leaves. These may indicate the presence of pests such as mealy bugs and red spider mites, which can still be active. Also clear up any fallen leaves and trim dead or damaged shoots as soon as you notice them.

The rest period is over at the first signs of new growth. Water the plant and, if appropriate, move it back into its preferred growing position in the house. This may also be a good time to repot (see page 42).

winter-flowering plants

Some winter-flowering houseplants and bulbs that have been forced for early flowers start their rest period as the days lengthen, rather than shorten. These include tulips, cyclamen, hippeastrums and Christmas cactus (*Schlumbergera*). Others – including *Jasminum polyanthum*, kalanchoe and *Primula obconica* – develop new growth in spring, and unusually their brief rest period coincides with their flowering one. In this case, plants should be kept cool and watered carefully. Always check a plant's winter preferences to avoid over-watering or keeping it at the wrong temperature.

21°C (70°F)
The maximum for most tender houseplants, like this *Begonia* Elatior hybrid, unless humidity is high.

Tender flowering plants such as this abutilon need to be kept in a frost-free environment, so move them away from windows at night-time during winter.

humidity & water

Water is vital to plant life. For healthy growth, humidity levels should be similar to those of a plant's natural habitat, and there must be adequate moisture supplied to its roots. It is important to know how much water each type of plant requires.

Humidity is a measure of the amount of moisture in the air at a given temperature. In centrally heated rooms the air can be very dry, with humidity levels as low as 15 per cent. Conditions like these are tolerated only by dry-air plants such as cacti and succulents, billbergias, spider plants (*Chlorophytum comosum*) and figs (*Ficus*). To prevent their leaves from drying out, most houseplants prefer humidity of 40–60 per cent – a range often found only in a bathroom or steamy kitchen. Fortunately, it is easy to increase humidity levels locally around a plant, by using any of the following techniques.

● **misting** Use a hand sprayer with a fine nozzle to mist leaf and stem surfaces in the morning, so they dry before nightfall. Do this daily in warm dry conditions. Misting will also discourage dust, as well as problems from red spider mite.

● **evaporation** Group plants that enjoy the same conditions in a tray or bowl filled with a layer of pebbles resting in a little water.

Plants can be grown together if they thrive in the same conditions. *Begonia rex*, syngonium, button fern (*Pellaea rotundifolia*), mind-your-own-business (*Soleirolia soleirolii*) and pogonatherum all like moist but well-drained soil and moderate humidity levels.

As the water evaporates, it will increase the humidity around the plants.

● **double potting** The evaporation effect can also be achieved by double potting: plunge the potted plant in an outer pot filled with moist gravel or vermiculite (see below left).

● **humidifiers** Installing a humidifier will raise the air moisture level in the whole room. A cheaper method is to stand a dish of water near a radiator and your plants.

Double potting helps to keep a plant moist. Select a container with a diameter about 5cm (2in) bigger than the pot in which the plant is growing. Half-fill the larger pot with gravel or vermiculite and then plunge in the planted pot and top up the gravel to the inner pot's rim. Regularly top up the water level in the gravel so the bottom third is damp.

Position the water meter half-way between the pot rim and the plant stems, here of a peace lily (right). Push the probe very gently into the compost until it is about two-thirds of the way down the pot, taking care not to damage any of the plant's roots or stems. Read the meter, then remove it and wipe clean.

When using a watering can to water hairy-leaved houseplants such as african violets (far right), hold back the foliage as it dislikes becoming wet. Do this gently as succulent leaves are very easy to break.

the importance of watering

Without water, plants die – quickly in the case of moisture lovers, such as peace lilies (*Spathiphyllum*) and some ferns, or over months, even years, for some drought-tolerant cacti and succulents. But over-watering commonly kills plants, too. Routine watering on a set day or at regular intervals can lead to over or under-watering, because needs vary according the time of year or stage of plant growth. It is much better to check all plants regularly and learn to judge when they need water and how much to give.

- **test the compost** by feeling if it is moist to the touch.
- **lift the pot** to see if it feels light and needs water, or is heavy and does not.
- **use a moisture meter**, or watering indicator that changes colour to give a warning reading.
- **look for early signs** that water is short, such as dull or pale leaf surfaces or slightly drooping buds and stem tips. Do not wait until plants wilt and stems become limp, as these are more advanced symptoms. If in doubt, wait a day rather than risk over-watering, which will unduly stress the plant. Roots in waterlogged compost will not be able to absorb oxygen from the atmosphere, which is needed for growth. In time the roots will start to rot and the plant will die.

how to water

Most plants prefer a good soak occasionally rather than frequent dribbles that do not wet all the compost and encourage the formation of roots close to the surface. Water the compost from above until excess begins to drip from the drainage hole. If water runs quickly through the pot, the compost is very dry and you should stand the plant in water until it is thoroughly moistened and bubbles cease to rise. Always consider whether a plant has special watering needs, such as the following.

- **plants that are resting**, or dormant, need very little water compared with those in flower or active growth.

- **plants in cool rooms** need less water than those in high temperatures.
- **hairy leaves** on plants such as gloxinias (*Sinningia speciosa*) and african violets (*Saintpaulia*) are damaged by water so a specific watering technique is needed (see above).
- **cacti and some other succulents** should be watered only sparingly.
- **bromeliads** such as aechmeas and vriesias like to have their central 'vase' filled with water (see page 130).
- **bog and water plants** such as cyperus and venus fly trap (*Dionaea*) need constant moisture.
- **air plants** absorb water vapour in humid air and so require regular misting instead of watering.

WATERING TIP Lime-hating plants such as azaleas (*Rhododendron simsii* hybrids) are best watered with rainwater, so collect some in a garden water butt. They must not be watered with tap water unless it is very soft or has been boiled and left to cool. Also, avoid using water from water-softeners, because it contains harmful chemicals.

Waterlogged plants can be slightly dried. Remove the plant (here crassula) carefully from its pot and wrap the rootball tightly in several layers of absorbent material, such as paper towels. Repeat until the excess moisture has been soaked up from the compost, then replace the plant carefully in its pot.

feeding

Plants require a variety of foods, including nitrogen, phosphorus, potassium and small quantities of many other minerals. Potting composts suitable for houseplants contain all these essential ingredients in carefully formulated mixtures, but this ready-made food supply does not last forever.

Potting composts contain only a limited amount of plant food, which quickly becomes used up by growing plants. The nutrients in soil-less composts normally last for about six to eight weeks, while those in soil-based mixtures linger slightly longer because the soil element also contains foods. After this, you need to start supplementary feeding if the plant is actively growing. Plants that are resting, or dormant, do not need food: unused fertiliser can accumulate in the potting compost, to possibly toxic levels.

dietary health check

Whenever you water your plants, assess their condition and learn to recognise the first signs of starvation or over-feeding before their health begins to suffer. Feeding is not a remedy for ill health and can actually make matters worse. Always check first for other possible causes, such as disease or being pot-bound, before assuming that a plant is suffering from starvation. After treating an ailing plant for a pest or disease problem, spray the leaves with a diluted liquid fertiliser, which can be absorbed quickly as a tonic if the plant needs it.

Yellowing leaves, as on this gardenia, are one sign of nutrient deficiency, but always check the plant for any other problems before treating it.

forms of fertiliser

Fertilisers are available in different formulations – some kinds specifically for indoor plants, while others are for general use in the garden. Always read the manufacturer's instructions to make sure the one you choose is appropriate.

Use specialist fertilisers for orchids, bromeliads, and cacti and other succulents. Foliage houseplants prefer a balanced fertiliser, whereas flowering houseplants will perform better if you feed them with one that is high in potash.

Plant food comes in many shapes and guises. Clockwise from bottom: fertiliser pins, clusters, concentrated liquid feed, ready-made liquid feed spikes and soluble powder feed.

● **concentrated liquid feeds**, soluble powders and crystals are the most convenient to use. The manufacturer's recommended amount is mixed into water and given to the plant at watering time. The same fertilisers but at greater dilutions can be sprayed on the leaves for very quick results. You need to repeat liquid feeding regularly, especially for very vigorous plants. Check the manufacturer's recommendations on feeding intervals, but also bear in mind the needs of each plant. Before applying liquid fertiliser,

top-dressing

Exhausted compost can be refreshed by top-dressing, which provides an immediate supply of nutrients in a layer of fresh compost. The technique is particularly good for large plants growing in pots 25cm (10in) or more in diameter, because they are difficult to repot. In general, the best time to top-dress is at the start of the growing season. Use an old table fork or a small scoop or trowel to remove a 2.5–5cm (1–2in) layer from the top of the old compost, taking care not to damage roots or stems. Replace with a layer of fresh compost, firm gently and water thoroughly.

make sure the compost is moist, as the roots can be burnt if conditions are dry.

● **clusters, pins and spikes** impregnated with fertiliser are pushed into the compost, where they remain active for up to a year, slowly dissolving whenever the plant is watered. Although convenient to handle, they tend to concentrate food in one part of the compost unless several are evenly distributed around the pot.

when to feed

Always check how often and how much food a particular houseplant needs. The majority of plants will stay healthy if fed regularly during the main growing season, from mid-spring to early autumn, but pay attention to the needs of particular plants. For example, a strongly growing busy lizzie (*Impatiens*) needs feeding every two to three weeks during spring and summer, while a less vigorous plant such as clivia can be happy with a single feed in spring and only two or three feeds in summer.

symptoms of under-feeding

● **upper leaves look small**, yellow, pale or lacklustre.
● **growth is slow**, weak or non-existent during the main growing season.
● **lower leaves turn yellow** and drop when growth should be active.
● **plants produce few or no blooms**, and these flowers are smaller than usual or malformed in some other way.

symptoms of over-feeding

● **stunted or twisted growth** occurs in summer, and thin weak stems develop in winter.
● **white crusty deposits** develop on the surface of potting compost and around the rim of clay pots.
● **unbalanced growth develops**, because a fertiliser stick or cluster has produced a concentration of food in one place, and so damaged nearby roots.
● **healthy leaves wilt**, but not owing to the plant being too dry or too wet.
● **leaf edges turn yellow or brown**, in combination with one or more of the above symptoms.

FEEDING TIP If a plant needs feeding when the compost is already very moist, apply a dilute foliar feed to the leaves or insert one or more fertiliser clusters in the potting compost. Either method avoids the risk of waterlogging the roots by adding yet more liquid.

Use a fertiliser high in potash for flowering plants (here *Hibiscus rosa-sinensis*), a cactus feed for cacti and other succulents, and a balanced fertiliser for foliage plants (here *Zamioculcas zamiifolia*).

training plants

Training can make the difference between a nondescript plant and a magnificent one. Many houseplants look more appealing if their growth is controlled as it develops. Training can also be used to encourage flowering, prolong a plant's life, or simply improve its shape by keeping it neatly within bounds.

Training is best done in early spring, when growth is rapid. The specific method used depends on the habit of the plant: bushy, climbing or trailing.

encouraging a bushy shape

Pinching out the growing tips on young stems of coleus (*Solenostemon*) and pelargoniums, for example, encourages more sideshoots and bushier growth. Unless training as a standard plant, pinch prune after a shoot has made about three leaves (see page 39), and repeat several times early in the season. This technique delays flowering, and should not be done when the main crop of flower buds appears.

Plants such as upright-growing figs (*Ficus*), oleander, cordyline and dracaena can become leggy on a single stem if left to their own devices. To avoid this, remove the tip of the main stem when it reaches 45–60cm (1½–2ft) in height. This will encourage branching from near the base, creating a bushier plant that will retain its lower leaves for longer.

training a standard

Shrubby plants such as fuchsias or heliotropes can be trained to form elegant standard plants with a tall single stem and bushy crown. Give the stem support right from the start, particularly for the trailing types of fuchsia, which will form a spectacular umbrella-like head but tend to have weak stems.

- **insert** a strong cane into the pot and secure the stem to the cane using string tied in a figure-of-eight.
- **check** the ties regularly as the shrub grows, and loosen any ties before they start to constrict the expanding stem.
- **remove** all sideshoots until the stem has reached the required height and then pinch out the tip.
- **allow** an evenly spaced framework of sideshoots to develop, usually about six to eight, and pinch out their tips when they are in balance with the main stem.

coping with climbers

Without regular attention to training, the shoots of climbers can grow very long and get into a terrible tangle. Training keeps the plants tidy but, more importantly, it also encourages flowering. When young, pliable-stemmed

Shrubby plants or stiff-stemmed climbers such as this bougainvillea look marvellous trained as a standard, with a clear main stem and the crown covered with flowers.

Indoor jasmine *Jasminum polyanthum* (left) is usually bought in late winter in full flower and trained around a hoop to keep its stems tidy.

climbers, such as jasmine, passion flower (*Passiflora*), wax flower (*Hoya*) and stephanotis, can be controlled by winding their stems around a wire or cane hoop. Climbers can also be grown through a wrought-iron support to make a screen or room divider. For this, the plants should ideally be grown in a long trough, but if this is not possible place individual pots close together. Suitable plants are cissus, ivies (*Hedera*) and philodendron. For the best effect use only one plant type. Stiff-stemmed climbers such as bougainvillea can be also trained as a standard (left).

For a few years, it is possible to continue winding and weaving pliable climber shoots around and through the hoop or room divider, but there comes a time when there is just too much growth. It becomes unwieldy and more permanent training becomes necessary over a more robust support. At this stage of maturity, it is best to tie the stems to horizontal wires or trellis fixed to a solid wall in a conservatory (right). To maximise flowering, train the stems horizontally and then downwards once they reach the top of the support.

moisture-loving climbers

Some tropical and sub-tropical climbers such as swiss cheese plant (*Monstera deliciosa*), epipremnums, syngoniums and philodendron produce aerial roots that, in the wild, are used to support and feed them as they grow through tall trees towards the light. These roots can look untidy but resist cutting them off. Instead, train the stems round a moss-covered pole. These are available from most garden centres, or make your own with a cylinder of wire netting filled with moss. Keep the pole moist by spraying. Tuck aerial roots into the moss or into the compost in the pot.

Ivy and other temperate plants with aerial roots can also be trained up moss or foam-covered poles.

trailing plants

For trailing houseplants such as tradescantia, space the stems evenly around the pot rim and allow them to extend to the desired length. Then pinch out the tips to encourage sideshoots, which can be pinch pruned in turn to produce bushy growth (see page 39).

training a permanent climber

1 **If a climber** grows top-heavy and too big for its support, as with this jasmine, untie the stems and remove the hoop or support wires. Do this after flowering and be very careful not to damage stems or leaves. Attach a strong trellis panel or a series of horizontal wires to a sunny wall indoors against which the climber can be trained.

2 **Cut back any** damaged, diseased or dead stems to healthy growth. Repot the plant in a container 5cm (2in) bigger in diameter than the previous pot, using John Innes No.2 compost. Place a larger outer container beside the sunny wall.

3 **Set the climber pot** inside the larger container and fill the gap with shingle for stability. If the outer pot has no drainage, first place a 2.5–5cm (1–2in) layer of shingle in the base. If you cannot attach trellis to a wall, insert the support in the shingle.

4 **Encourage the** stems of the newly pruned and repotted plant to climb the trellis by tying the stems to the supports. Continue to train and tie in the new shoots as they appear.

houseplant grooming

A small amount of effort on a regular basis pays huge dividends with houseplants. Just cleaning and tidying will keep most healthy and looking good, although many also benefit from a certain amount of pruning and further training to keep them in good shape and acceptable size.

grooming

Regular deadheading, training and leaf cleaning do much to improve the looks of houseplants. Deadheading – the removal of dying or dead flowers – encourages some plants to produce more blooms, particularly african violets (*Saintpaulia*), streptocarpus and seed-raised pelargoniums. When deadheading wax flowers (*Hoya*) and any other plants that produce permanent flower stalks, take care not to remove the stalks, as doing so will reduce future flowering.

After initial training (see page 36), continue tying in new shoots of houseplants and replace any ties that have deteriorated or are restricting growth. Also, tuck in aerial roots on moisture-loving climbers such as swiss cheese plant (*Monstera deliciosa*) and epipremnum.

Grooming tasks during the growing season include pinch pruning young shoots – also referred to as stopping – on plants that are grown for their attractive foliage. This encourages a bushy shape by stimulating sideshoots to develop and preventing the formation of flower buds. On soft stems, just remove the growing tip with a finger and thumb; for tough woody stems, use a pair of sharp scissors or a pruning knife. Regular pinch pruning is particularly important for trailing plants, which can otherwise become long and leggy with leaves mainly towards the growing tip.

cleaning

Household dust makes foliage look tired and dirty. Worse, if allowed to accumulate it can block the breathing pores in leaves and prevent maximum daylight from reaching the surface. Remove most of the dust while it is dry, using a soft paintbrush or shaving brush. This is the only way to clean hairy leaves. Shiny foliage, however, can then be washed and polished. Wipe large leaves with a sponge or lint-free cloth. Proprietary wipes are also available. Be especially gentle with plants such as stag's horn fern (*Platycerium*), as the leaves have a waxy coat, which should not be removed.

For an authentic shine, and to avoid the unnatural appearance often given by leaf polishes, clean leaves (here of medinilla) with a little warmed milk. Use only a light touch when wiping each leaf.

The best way to remove dust from plants with numerous small leaves is to stand them outdoors in gentle rain or spray them with clean water. Do this early in the day so plants have time to dry off before nightfall.

grooming techniques

Deadhead plants regularly by nipping off dead flowers (here of african violet) or cutting the flower stems at the base, using a pair of scissors.

Tie trailing stems (here of wax flower) to a wire hoop or other support using string tied in a figure-of-eight, so that the stems do not rub against the support.

Tuck in aerial roots, here of swiss cheese plant, while they are still young and pliable, so they do not become damaged. If necessary, secure them with string wound in a figure-of-eight and then tied.

Cut back thin, leggy stems about 5mm (¼in) above a healthy leaf bud, or node. Sharp secateurs will cut pencil-thick stems. For thicker ones, use long-handled pruners.

pruning

Mature leggy plants can be much improved by pruning out weak or over-long stems. This minor pruning can be done at any time and promotes a burst of young growth from near the base of the plant.

More drastic pruning, when a large proportion of old growth is removed to encourage good shape and vigour, is best undertaken in spring, just as growth begins and before repotting, should this be necessary (see page 42). Cut back hard all, or nearly all, the old stems, and prune out dead, damaged and straggly growth. Then thin crowded and crossing stems, and shorten all remaining main stems by up to half, cutting just above a bud or a strong new shoot.

Pruning tools should be very sharp and clean. Woody stems should be cut with secateurs or long-handled pruners, according to the thickness of the stem, while dense bushy growth can be removed with pointed scissors, and soft shoots with a pruning knife or pinched out between finger and thumb.

- **untie climbers** such as jasmine and passion flowers (*Passiflora*) before shortening older stems.
- **over-tall single-stemmed** plants such as rubber plants (*Ficus elastica*) or dracaenas can be cut 1m (3ft) or more below their tips; new growth will appear after a few weeks.
- **philodendron and ivies** (*Hedera*) can produce thin, almost leafless shoots in winter, and these need to be pruned back to their point of origin in spring.

PRUNING EUPHORBIAS TIP Euphorbias discharge a toxic milky sap after pruning. Protect your hands with rubber gloves, and reduce the flow of sap by covering the cut surface with fine charcoal or ash.

A good example of a well-groomed plant is this *Exacum affine* 'White Midget'. Its bushy shape has been achieved by the regular pinch pruning of non-flowering shoots, and its clean glossy leaves proclaim its good health.

Pinch prune the growing tips on young stems (here of tradescantia) using a finger and thumb. Remove the tip just above a leaf joint where the uppermost leaf or pair of leaves emerge.

keeping plants healthy

Houseplants suffer from fewer problems than plants growing outdoors, and any pest or disease symptoms are usually noticed at an early stage. If you inspect plants regularly, disorders can be identified and treated before they become serious.

pests and diseases

The main source of pest and disease infection is from new plants when they are brought into the house, so check plants thoroughly before buying. Houseplants that have spent the summer outside also need careful inspection before bringing inside, and any dead or dying foliage should be removed. Always wash the outsides of pots before giving them a place indoors. If you can see signs of pests on a plant, pick or wash them off, or spray with an insecticide, then quarantine the plant for a week or two before mixing it with others.

When a houseplant is infected with a pest or disease, treat it promptly because a problem can quickly spread in congenial indoor surroundings. Always use a product suitable for houseplants and follow meticulously the manufacturer's instructions.

Treat infested plants with a systemic insecticidal spray. For safety, do this in an isolated spot outside, away from other plants. If you have to spray indoors, wrap a plastic bag round the plant to create a closed environment, as with this weeping fig (*Ficus benjamina*), and make sure the room is well ventilated.

common pests

The most frequently found pests include:

- **aphids** Tiny soft-bodied insects, often found in colonies on shoot tips and the undersides of leaves. Sponge off with water or an insecticidal soap solution, or spray with an insecticide.
- **caterpillars** Tell-tale signs include partly eaten leaves and dark droppings. These pests often cling to the undersides of leaves, and can be picked off by hand and destroyed.
- **red spider mite** Minute insects that turn leaves yellow or mottled, eventually covering them with fine webbing. They like dry conditions and are often resistant to chemicals. Spray or wipe leaves with an insecticidal soap solution and increase humidity by misting or other means (see page 32).
- **mealy bugs** Patches of white fluff conceal these tiny greyish insects. Spray with an insecticidal soap every two weeks until clear of infestation.
- **scale insects** Small raised blisters hide and protect these tiny insects, often found along stems and veins on the underside of leaves. Wipe off scales with a cottonbud.
- **vine weevils** These white grubs feed on roots so the plant wilts, while dark adult weevils eat notches from the leaf edges. Both are difficult to control. Search out and destroy

Clean the outside of plant pots that have spent the summer outside before bringing them indoors. This group includes busy lizzie (*Impatiens*), shrimp plant (*Justicia brandegeeana*) and stromanthe.

grubs among the roots, then repot in fresh potting compost, or water plants with a biological control (*Heterorhabditis*) when the temperature is 12°C (54°F) or more.

diseases

Serious diseases are rare but often difficult to treat, so it is better to discard badly affected plants. Isolate a diseased plant immediately and check others frequently for symptoms.

● **rotting or decayed stems** Usually the result of excessive watering, especially in autumn and winter when plants need less water. Plants can sometimes be saved by cutting out affected areas and drying out the compost (see page 33).

● **moulds and mildews** Fluffy or powdery, white or grey patches occur in moist or cool conditions. Treat by removing infected foliage and spraying with an appropriate fungicide.

other problems

One of the most common problems is overwatering rather than under-watering. Symptoms of this include wilting flowers and buds falling off, and pale or brown-edged leaves.

Ill health may also be caused by draughts or fluctuating temperatures, insufficient light or too much direct sun, or the wrong humidity level. Hard water can cause the leaves of lime-hating plants such as azaleas to turn yellow.

Adjusting the growing conditions can often lead to prompt recovery, so review your care of a plant before assuming it is diseased. Bear in mind, however, that some plants, including annuals and bulbs, and older stems of bromeliads and cyperus, naturally die down after flowering, and some leaves of evergreens turn yellow and brown with increasing age.

Yellowing or unsightly damaged or dead foliage (here on a cyclamen) should be promptly pulled away, or cut with sharp scissors, as it can harbour disease.

Scale insects (here on *Aloe vera*) are one of the most common houseplant pests, particularly those with leathery or succulent leaves, and cacti. Remove them with a cottonbud and isolate the affected plant from its neighbours, which you should check regularly in case the pest has spread.

holiday care

Before you go away, especially during summer, ask someone to look after your houseplants and leave a note of any special treatments that might be needed. If you have to leave the plants completely unattended, move them away from sunny windows and remove all flowers and buds. Keep the compost moist by using self-watering pots, watering wicks or capillary mats. To set up a mat, place flat-bottomed pots with drainage holes on an upturned seed tray covered with a capillary mat (left). Keep the mat wet by trailing one end into a container with water in it. Raise the container initially so that the water level is above that of the pot bases, but once the water is flowing, lower the water level.

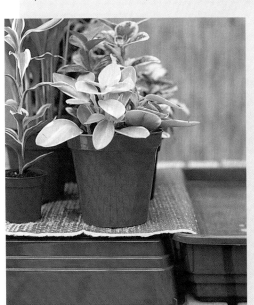

Alternatively, water the plants thoroughly, gather them together in a sink or bath, and pack wet screwed-up newspaper between the pots to create a moist microclimate. During winter, when most plants are relatively inactive, ensure the compost is moist, then position plants away from windows and draughts, in a temperature just above their preferred minimum.

repotting

For the best results, most houseplants require repotting into fresh potting compost, and possibly into a larger pot, from time to time. How often this needs to be done depends on the plant's rate of growth and on the condition of its potting compost.

reasons for repotting

If your houseplants are growing well, they are likely at some point to show signs of needing more space for their roots. Symptoms include:

- **very slow growth** even when fed regularly;
- **compost dries out quickly** and needs watering frequently;
- **roots appear** at the surface or through drainage holes;
- **green algae** develops on the compost surface.

To check whether repotting is required, water the plant and leave it to drain. Then place the pot on its side and gently knock its rim to loosen the rootball. Spreading your fingers over the compost surface and round the plant's stem, remove the plant from the pot. If there is a mass of roots covering the compost and often winding round the bottom of the pot, the plant is pot-bound and needs repotting into fresh compost and possibly a larger container. This is best done in spring or at the start of the plant's growing season.

REPOTTING TIP Do not assume a plant needs repotting or potting on just because it looks too large for its pot. Many houseplants enjoy confined conditions, especially if fed regularly, and should be disturbed only if they become pot-bound.

Algae growing on the surface of potting compost is a sign that the plant may be pot-bound and need repotting.

choosing a pot size

An established plant is generally repotted in fresh potting compost within the same-sized pot, and up to one-third of its roots are pruned to prevent it being pot-bound. You can either use a new pot or scrub clean the original one very thoroughly inside and out.

If you want your plant to grow bigger, pot it on into a slightly larger container, about 2.5–5cm (1–2in) wider. Follow the same procedure as for repotting (see left), but cover the drainage material with fresh compost before positioning the plant in the pot.

choosing a potting compost

To work efficiently any planting medium has to drain well, yet absorb enough water to prevent a plant from drying out too quickly. It also needs a sufficiently firm texture to hold the plant upright, and should ideally contain a supply of plant food. Garden soil may possess these qualities, but it also contains weed seeds and pests, and may have the wrong chemical or physical structure. Therefore, dedicated potting composts are used instead. There are two main types.

repotting a plant

1 Remove the plant from its pot and discard the drainage material. Carefully use your fingers or a plant label to tease about 1cm (½in) of old compost away from the roots. Then cut away any dead or damaged roots, and any coiled round the base of the rootball.

2 Lay fresh drainage material in the bottom of a clean pot and centre the plant in it, with the surface at the same level as before. Fill round the rootball with fresh compost, working it between the roots with your fingers. Tap the pot to settle the contents, level the surface and trim back some of the top growth to balance any root pruning. Water the plant thoroughly.

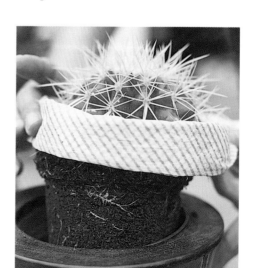

When repotting prickly plants such as cacti, wrap a long strip of folded cloth or paper around the plant. Hold the free ends like a handle and lift the plant clear of its pot.

- **soil-based potting compost**, usually made to the John Innes (JI) recipe, is a mixture of loam (good-quality sterilised soil), coarse sand, peat substitute or peat, and fertiliser. It does not exhaust its food reserves nor dry out quickly, but it may vary in quality. JI composts are relatively heavyweight, although this can provide stability for top-heavy plants.
- **soil-less potting compost** is increasingly made from a peat substitute such as coir or composted bark, although traditionally it is made of peat. It is naturally low in nutrients and easy to over-water; also it can be difficult to re-wet if allowed to dry out. Being lightweight, it does not provide such a stable roothold as a soil-based compost.

special potting composts

These are available for particular houseplants and purposes.
- **ericaceous compost**, sometimes called rhododendron compost, is a lime-free mix for acid-loving houseplants such as azaleas and heathers (*Erica*).
- **bulb fibre** is a coarse soil-less compost with added charcoal which keeps the compost 'sweet' and prevents the roots rotting. It is suitable for pots without drainage holes.
- **seed compost** contains few nutrients. It is for sowing and raising seedlings.

- **cuttings compost** includes grit or perlite for good drainage, to help cuttings develop roots without rotting.
- **special blends of potting composts** are available for bonsai, bromeliads, cacti, ferns and orchids.

drainage materials

One of the most common reasons for a plant to fail is because it is struggling in waterlogged compost. This problem can be greatly reduced by placing a layer of coarse drainage material in the base of the pot. Suitable materials include crocks (pieces of clay pot), gravel, pebbles, broken bricks and pieces of polystyrene. Provide a 1cm (½in) layer in pots up to 12cm (5in) in diameter, and 2.5cm (1in) for larger pots. Cacti and succulents need a layer of gravel, up to 5cm (2in) thick, beneath the gritty cactus compost.

types of potting compost

Here are just some examples of the many different kinds of potting compost available.

Soil-less mix
(for *Aphelandra squarrosa*)

Cacti mix
(for *Pilosocereus*)

Ericaceous mix
(for azaleas)

Bonsai mix
(for *Tsuga canadensis*)

Orchid mix
(for *Phalaenopsis*)

hydroculture

This is a very precise and straightforward alternative method of growing houseplants. Instead of compost as the medium in which plants root, modern hydroculture uses sterile clay granules in water to support plants and give them an oxygen-rich rooting environment.

The simplest form of hydroculture, or water culture, can be demonstrated by growing a hyacinth or sweet potato in a bulb glass filled with water. The bulb lives off its food reserves to develop roots and a flower.

Other plants can also be grown 'hydroponically', but they need a more sophisticated approach with nutrient-rich water and inert aggregates that provide support. The most widely used aggregates are porous clay granules. These absorb nutrients and large amounts of oxygen for the plant roots, which are not submerged in the water.

growing plants in water

Hydroculture can relieve the need for regular watering, especially if you go away on holiday. It is particularly suitable for plant cuttings rooted in water, because no period of adjustment is needed when they are moved into pots, as there would be if the rooted cuttings were transplanted into potting compost.

The hydroponic growing technique is also simple to use – a special water indicator changes colour when the water is low. Fertiliser is added whenever the water level is topped up, using one of two special formulations for either flowering or foliage plants.

A compost-based plant takes a few weeks to adapt to hydroculture, while it develops a different kind of root system.

houseplants suitable for hydroculture

These are some of the more popular houseplants suitable for hydroculture, but many more can thrive in water and it is well worth experimenting.

- african violet (*Saintpaulia*) ● *Anthurium* ● bulbs
- cape primrose (*Streptocarpus*) ● *Cissus*
- croton (*Codiaeum*) ● devil's ivy (*Epipremnum*)
- *Dracaena* ● dumb cane (*Dieffenbachia*) (left)
- ivy (*Hedera*) ● peace lily (*Spathiphyllum*)
- *Schefflera* ● sweet potato (*Ipomoea battata*)
- *Tradescantia* ● umbrella plant (*Cyperus involucratus*) ● weeping fig (*Ficus benjamina*)

Cyperus and colourful croton
can be grown together using hydroculture. Such a combination is unlikely to work in potting compost.

choosing containers

Traditionally, hydroculture used a special two-part container with an inner perforated pot that held a plant surrounded by aggregate. The inner pot was suspended over a large outer one, which held a fertiliser solution. This seeped into the aggregate in the inner pot by capillary action and so nourished the houseplant.

With modern hydroculture, only one container is needed. Any style is suitable as long as the pot is clean, watertight and holds about twice the volume of a pot in which an equivalent soil-based plant might be grown. Glass pots or jars allow you to watch root development, and clay granules can look attractive in

Stems of dracaena will root in water. When the root system is well developed, plant the cuttings in clay granules, as demonstrated below.

them. Opaque containers, however, are preferable for long-term plants, because roots develop better in the dark.

regular maintenance

Only when the water gauge indicator reverts to its original 'dry' colour does a plant need water. Pour in a quarter of the pot's capacity of water mixed with the same type of liquid fertiliser as previously. Once or twice a year, replace the water completely, to prevent a build-up of waste products.

As plants grow they will need moving to a larger container. Fortunately, the granules can be used again and again, providing you wash them thoroughly and let them dry between 'pottings'.

potting plants in clay granules

1 Measure how much water the container holds and note this down for future reference. Then fill the bottom one-third of the container with clay granules. In a bucket, gently wash off any debris or old compost from the roots, here of anthurium.

2 Position the plant on the granules in the container and spread out its roots evenly. Trickle in more granules until the plant is securely anchored with the base of its stem about level with the granules.

3 Pour one-quarter of the container's capacity of water – enriched with the appropriately formulated fertiliser – over the granules. Insert a watering gauge down into the root area, taking care not to damage the roots and making sure that the gauge indicator is visible. Then check that the gauge shows 'wet'. If it does not, push the gauge further down into the root area. Then read the gauge again.

4 If the plant was previously growing in clay granules, set its container in a suitably lit position in the house or conservatory. However, plants that were previously planted in potting compost need to be kept shaded, warm and humid in a propagator or sealed plastic bag. Once you can see new succulent roots growing, remove the covering and put the plant in appropriate light.

forcing houseplants

Forcing is the art of artificially inducing bulbs and other plants and vegetables into early growth. It allows you to enjoy fresh, cheerful daffodils at Christmas, and crunchy chicory throughout the winter months.

Normally if you plant bulbs or other plants in pots and stand them outside, they will flower at the same time as if they were growing in a bed or border. However, you can get them to bloom earlier and cheer the midwinter gloom by forcing the plants into earlier growth. As well as bulbs, a great variety of other plants including pinks (*Dianthus*) and lily-of-the-valley (*Convallaria*) are suitable for forcing, and many of them are sweetly scented (see page 128).

planning your display

You can either buy bulbs that are ready prepared for forcing – they will have been temperature-treated by the grower to speed up flowering – or you can force your own bulbs. Choose early flowering varieties and plant them between August and October; for Christmas blooms, plant in September. The bulbs should start flowering 12–15 weeks after planting, according to type – narcissi and hyacinths take about 12 weeks, and other bulbs a little longer. For a continuous show of flowers through winter, plant up bowls at 2–3 week intervals.

Avoid mixing different bulb types in the same container, or even different varieties of the same bulb, because they will flower at varying times and the display will look untidy. If you want a mixed display, pot up and force each bulb individually. Then pick out those that have buds showing colour, and that are obviously at the same flowering stage, to combine in a bowl for a mixed display.

after flowering

Remove the flower heads when they start to fade, but not the stalks. Move the bowl to a cool room or coldframe; continue to water and feed with a high-potash fertiliser until the leaves yellow. Then either plant the bulbs intact in the garden or dry and store them in a cool dark place over summer, planting them in the garden in autumn. Bulbs forced for indoor decoration should not be used a second year as houseplants, but most will flower outside – if rather sparsely – in the first spring after replanting in the garden.

A glorious indoor display of *Narcissus* 'Tête-à-tête' and yellow *Iris danfordiae*) is bright and colourful. Discard 'Tête-à-tête' bulbs after flowering, and plant irises outside in the garden.

bulb varieties

suitable for forcing

- amaryllis (*Hippeastrum*)
- *Crocus chrysanthus*
- *Crocus tommasinianus*
- *Cyclamen persicum*
- dutch hyacinths such as *Hyacinthus orientalis* 'Jan Bos' and 'Pink Pearl'
- early tulips such as 'Peach Blossom' (double) and 'Princess Margaret' (single) • lilies (*Lilium*)
- snowdrops (*Galanthus*)
- tazetta narcissi, such as paper-white narcissus (*N. papyraceus*)

forcing vegetables indoors

Roots of chicory and rhubarb can be dug up from the garden and forced indoors in a dark cupboard or covered with an upturned pot (with drainage hole blocked) to keep out the light.

- **chicory** Dig up roots in autumn or winter. Trim away all but 2.5cm (1in) of the foliage and remove the root tip. Plant in a deep pot, leaving the root tops slightly exposed above the compost. Leave in the dark at room temperature for about six weeks.
- **rhubarb** Dig up roots in late autumn and leave exposed to frost on the soil surface for 2–3 weeks. Then pot them up in a large container, such as a 25cm (10in) pot or bucket. Keep in the dark at about 10°C (50°F) and water occasionally. Juicy tender stems will be ready for picking in about six weeks. In spring, return the roots to the garden, replanting in soil that has been enriched with well-rotted manure or garden compost.

forcing bulbs

To force bulbs for indoors, spread a generous layer of damp bulb fibre in the base of a shallow bowl. If using a different type of potting compost, include a drainage layer (see page 43).

- Place the bulbs on top and fill round them with more damp bulb fibre. Press down the fibre firmly. If there is space, top-dress with moss or pretty stones.
- Cover the bowls in black plastic bags and stand them in an area where the temperature does not rise above 4°C (40°F), such as a shed, unheated greenhouse, coldframe or garage.
- Check occasionally to see how the shoots are developing and that the bulb fibre is not drying out.
- When the shoots reach 2.5–5cm (1–2in), bring the bowls indoors. Keep them in a cool place out of direct sunlight until the shoots begin to turn green, then move them to a position with more light.
- When the flower buds start to show, transfer the bowl into its flowering position, preferably a bright spot where the temperature does not exceed 20°C (68°F).
- Water as necessary and use thin canes to support the flowers as they open. Feed weekly with a high-potash houseplant fertiliser.

Bulbs should be planted close together but not touching, and the tip of each bulb should just show above the bulb fibre.

forcing chicory

1 **Fill a 25cm (10in) pot** with moist potting compost. Insert three trimmed roots upright. Cover the pot and leave in the dark.

2 **Blanched chicory heads** will develop from the planted roots and should be ready to harvest after about six weeks.

propagating plants

The ability to reproduce your own plants is a rewarding skill to acquire, and will give you plenty of new vigorous houseplants as well as some to give away to friends. Most plants are easy to propagate, providing you use the most appropriate technique.

ways to propagate

There are four basic ways to reproduce houseplants – by seed, layering, division and cuttings. Many plants can be propagated by more than one technique, and you will need to choose the best method for your situation.

With houseplants, when to propagate is determined more by the state of the plant than by the season. A vigorous, healthy parent plant will produce vigorous sturdy offspring at any time. That said, spring and early summer, when plants grow strongly, are usually the best times for propagation, although some seed may be sown at other times of year.

Shake fern fronds bearing ripe spore cases into a paper bag, then scatter them thinly over the surface of a small plastic pot filled with soil-less seed compost. Cover the pot with a sheet of glass or seal it in a clear polythene bag. When the young plants are large enough to handle, plant them singly in small pots.

sowing seed

Certain houseplants grow better from seed than using any other form of propagation. These are mainly the quick-growing ones that are often discarded after their first season, such as black-eyed susans (*Thunbergia alata*), coleus (*Solenostemon*), busy lizzies (*Impatiens*) and polka dot plants (*Hypoestes phyllostachya*). Early flowering houseplants such as polyanthus also grow better from seed. Ferns produce dust-like spores on the under-surfaces of some fronds, and these spores can be 'sown' (above right).

Sowing seed is an easy job to do, but for best results use a covered propagator with a thermostatically controlled heating element to maintain the correct temperature.
● Fill a small clean shallow pot or seed tray with damp seed compost. Sow seeds thinly on top, covering all but very fine seeds with their own depth of compost. Bury large seeds in compost.
● Stand in a propagator, or put into a clear polythene bag secured with a rubber band. Place in a shady spot at a temperature of 15–21°C (60–70°F).

● As soon as the seeds have germinated, remove the polythene cover to give them more light (not direct sunlight). Turn the pot round a little each day to prevent the seedlings becoming 'leggy'.
● When the seedlings are large enough to handle, prick them out into small pots filled with potting compost and grow on.

layering

Layering encourages roots to form where a stem that is still attached to the parent plant has been artifically wounded, or nicked.
● **in simple layering** (top right), the stem is brought down to the compost so the wound can be buried. This technique is suitable for propagating climbing or trailing houseplants, such as ivy (*Hedera*) and philodendron.
● **in air layering** (far right), the compost is brought up to the wound on the stem, which is then wrapped in polythene. This technique is suitable for thick-stemmed houseplants, such as devil's ivy (*Epipremnum aureum*) and rubber plant (*Ficus elastica*), particularly those plants that have become unshapely with age.

You can use air layering to create new plants from older ones that may have grown too tall for their surroundings. The rubber plant (right) can be propagated in this way.

Position large seeds individually on the surface of the potting compost, spacing them evenly. Gently push each seed into the soil until it is buried under its own depth of compost.

simple layering

Fill a clean plant pot with moist cuttings compost and place it beside the parent plant (here an ivy). To encourage rooting, make a slanted nick in the underside of a strong-growing, flexible stem on the parent plant. Bury the nicked part of the stem in the compost, pinning it in position with a bent piece of wire or a hairpin. Keep the compost moist, and roots will form where the stem is pinned down. When this occurs, the new plant can be cut free from its parent.

air layering

1 **Choose a** 10cm (4in) section of stem no more than 60cm (2ft) from the tip of the plant (here, devil's ivy) and remove any leaves on it. Make a shallowly angled nick, about 1cm (½in) long, into the bare stem, below a leaf junction.

2 **At the bottom** of the bare stem section, tie or tape a polythene bag or other transparent wrapping around the stem, then fold it back downwards, out of the way. Dust the wound with rooting hormone, using a paintbrush.

3 **Work damp** peat substitute or sphagnum moss into the wound, using the back of a knife. Then roll the polythene wrapping up into position around the wounded part of the stem, and fill it with more damp peat substitute or sphagnum moss.

4 **Tie or tape** the top of the polythene wrapping around the stem. After about two months, roots should be visible through the polythene. Sever the rooted layer from the parent plant below the bottom tie, unwrap it and pot it up.

propagating plants/2

division

Dividing is a common way to increase many houseplants. There are three main ways to do this.

• **in division of rootstock**, an established plant can be increased by splitting its rootball into several smaller pieces, each with a fat, healthy bud or shoot, and potting them up individually (below right). Position the newly potted sections in good light, and water sparingly until they produce fresh growth. Many clump-forming houseplants, such as prayer plants (*Maranta*), stromanthe and some ferns, can be propagated in this way, as can some houseplants that separate into a number of rosettes, such as african violets (*Saintpaulia*) and ctenanthe.

• **some houseplants produce baby plants** which can be detached and planted individually

in a small pot of multipurpose potting compost, if they have well-developed roots. Pick-a-back plants (*Tolmiea*) develop them on their leaves, while mother of thousands (*Saxifraga stolonifera*) and spider plants (*Chlorophytum comosum*) grow baby plants at the end of long stems. If there are no roots, pin the baby plant into the compost while still attached to the stem (above).

• **offsets, or sideshoots**, are another type of plantlet produced from the main plant. These can be detached and potted up individually, whether they have roots or not (below left). This is the best way to propagate many cacti, bromeliads, aloes and sansevierias.

With a bent piece of wire, pin down each baby plant (here of spider plant) into a pot filled with moist potting compost.

Before splitting the offsets away from the parent, first water the plant and then remove it from its pot. Gently prise the offsets (here of *Aloe vera*) away from the rootball. Plant them up in their own individual pots and grow on.

division of rootstock

1 **Water the plant** (here stromanthe), then remove it from its pot. Divide the rootball into sections, each with a portion of roots as well as a bud or young shoot, if necessary using a sharp knife.

2 **Pot up each section** in a pot of suitable size filled with cuttings compost. Work the compost between the roots, firm gently and water well. Place in a well-lit position while the new plant becomes established.

Slashed leaf cutting
Cut through the main veins on the back of a *Begonia rex* leaf (above). Lie the leaf on the compost surface, facing upwards, and weight it in place with small stones (right).

types of leaf cuttings

Stalked leaf cutting Shorten each leaf stalk (here african violet) to 3.5–5cm (1½–2in). Make a hole for each cutting and insert each stalk so the leaf base is just above the compost. Firm the compost around each stalk.

Midrib leaf cutting Cut a leaf (here cape primrose) in half and remove the main vein. Insert each leaf half, cut side down into cuttings compost. Plantlets will develop along the cut leaf edge.

cuttings

Most houseplants can be propagated by taking cuttings from a healthy leaf or stem.

● **leaf cuttings** (see above) Some houseplants, such as african violets (*Saintpaulia*) and gloxinias (*Sinningia speciosa*), can be propagated from a stalked leaf. Certain stemless plants can be raised from just the leaf either by cutting it along the midrib, as for many succulents, sansevieria and cape primroses (*Streptocarpus*), or by slashing the main veins, as in foliage begonias. The leaf cutting will gradually decay as the new plants develop along its cut edges.

Once you have taken leaf cuttings, water them and place the pot in a shaded propagator or under a sealed polythene covering, at a temperature of 18°C (65°F) until new growth appears. When the new plants are large enough to handle, transplant them into individual containers and grow on.

● **stem cuttings** A shoot, 8–15cm (3–6in) long with its growing tip, is cut off the parent plant and inserted into moist cuttings compost, where it will develop roots. Many houseplants can be increased in this way – not only shrubby plants such as hibiscus and abutilon but also soft-stemmed houseplants, such as tradescantia. Early in the growing season, use vigorous, young, soft-stemmed shoots, with the lower leaves removed, as cuttings. Woodier shoots can be used in summer or autumn.

● **cane cuttings** Plants with cane-like stems – for example, cordyline and dracaena – can be propagated from pieces of stem, each 5–8cm (2–3in) long and with at least one leaf bud. The cuttings are either laid horizontally in a small pot of cuttings compost with the leaf bud facing upwards, or are inserted vertically. In either case the leaf bud, from which the new plant will develop, must be covered with compost.

taking stem cuttings

1 **Fill a pot** 15cm (6in) in diameter with cuttings compost and firm gently to leave about 1cm (½in) space at the top for watering. Take young vigorous cuttings 8–15cm (3–6in) long, depending on the plant (here fuchsia). Cut straight across the bottom below a leaf joint, and remove any leaves from the lower half of the cutting. Make holes and insert up to six cuttings around the edge of the container. Water the cuttings in lightly.

2 **Cover the pot** with a clear plastic bag, held away from the leaves with 3–4 canes and secured at the base with a rubber band. Alternatively, stand the pot in a heated propagator, set at 18°C (65°F), until the cuttings root. When new leaves appear, remove the cover and water. Then pot on the rooted cuttings into individual small pots of multipurpose compost.

Pot plants come in all types and sizes, from flowering annuals that bring temporary colour into the home, to large long-lived plants that provide year-round foliage and structure. Although many indoor plants are bought on impulse, if you are shopping for a new houseplant it does help to have some idea of what type is needed. This directory describes over one hundred plant groups (genera) and provides a selection of plants that are reliable and widely available. If you cannot find a selected plant, your garden centre may be able to recommend an alternative. Remember that garden centres regularly take fresh deliveries of plants, and that many flowering types are seasonal and offered for sale only as they are coming into bloom.

plant selector

Gerbera jamesonii cultivar

Cultivation notes

Accompanying each plant is a guide to its preferred growing conditions, which will help you to decide whether it is likely to thrive in your home.

General care: Tips on repotting, pruning and other reminders to help you keep plants in good shape.

Height and spread: The figures refer to an average mature specimen, but depend on growing conditions and any pruning that may have been done.

Temperature: Most of the plants featured are happy at normal room temperatures of 18–24°C (65–75°F) (see page 30).

Humidity: The level of moisture in the air may become an issue when temperatures increase; for tips on improving humidity see page 32.

Light: As the foliage of many plants may be damaged by the effect of direct sun through glass, bright indirect light is preferred (see page 28). This can be filtered through a net or voile curtain or found away from a window. East and west-facing windows, which receive direct sun only early or late in the day, are suitable for many species.

Watering: This is the most critical aspect of houseplant care (see page 33). Most plants can be watered freely while they are growing in summer, so the compost is kept constantly and evenly moist. Moderate watering allows the compost to dry out somewhat between applications and is the best way to treat plants during the other seasons. Plants from arid climates need to be watered sparingly, so the compost almost dries out between watering, especially in winter when growth has all but stopped.

Feeding: Unnecessary for temporary pot plants such as chrysanthemums, but longer-lived plants benefit from feeding while they grow (see page 34).

Propagation: The easiest methods of propagating are given here; more details on techniques are on pages 48–51.

Pests and diseases: The most likely pests and diseases are listed (see also page 40).

Good companions: Plants with similar cultural needs make the best neighbours.

abutilon

Abutilons are soft-woody shrubs that intermittently produce bell-shaped flowers from spring to autumn. Although widely distributed throughout tropical and sub-tropical regions, most of those grown as houseplants are large-bloomed hybrids raised by plant breeders. Left unpruned, abutilons make twiggy shrubs 2m (6ft) or more tall, but will form bushy plants if cut back to a good framework each spring and any over-long shoots shortened.

A. hybrids
These evergreen or semi-evergreen shrubs bear pendent white, pink, yellow or red blooms with prominent orange or yellow stamens. Good varieties include yellow-flowered 'Canary Bird', white 'Boule de Neige' and scarlet 'Ashford Red'. Some have variegated foliage.

A. megapotamicum
The yellow flowers of this trailing evergreen or semi-evergreen shrub emerge from a red, lantern-shaped calyx.

A. pictum 'Thompsonii'
The yellow mottling of this evergreen plant's intricately shaped leaves are caused by a harmless virus. The flowers are apricot in colour.

General care: Repot every spring. Prune in spring. If a plant becomes too spindly, take cuttings to create new plants and discard the parent. May be stood outdoors in summer.

Height: 1m (3ft) **Spread:** 75cm (2½ft)

Temperature: Normal room

Humidity: Not fussy

Light: Bright, including direct sun

Watering: Freely while in active growth in summer, sparingly in winter

Feeding: Monthly from spring to late summer

Propagation: Stem cuttings between spring and late summer

Pests and diseases: Aphids, red spider mite

Good companions: *Hibiscus rosa-sinensis* cultivars, *Iresine herbstii* cultivars

Abutilon 'Canary Bird'

agave

Slow-growing evergreen succulents with leaves usually arranged in a rosette, agaves make good foliage plants for a sunny windowsill but are unlikely to flower indoors. They associate well with other succulents and cacti, and look particularly good in terracotta pots top-dressed with gravel. Originally from dry regions of the Americas, they do not need much water, except in summer, to encourage growth and the development of a well-shaped plant.

Agave filifera

A. filifera Thread agave
This slow-growing evergreen succulent forms a rosette of spine-tipped leaves. White threads curl away from the leaf margins.

A. parryi
The broad, blue-green leaves are armed with vicious spines.

A. victoriae-reginae Queen Victoria century plant, Royal agave
This forms a neat dome of spine-tipped leaves that are marked with white. New rosettes may form around the base.

General care: May be placed outdoors in summer. Use gritty free-draining compost when repotting (every few years).

Height and spread: 20–50cm (8–20in)

Temperature: Normal room, minimum 5°C (41°F)

Humidity: Dry air, but tolerates humid air

Light: Bright, including direct sun

Watering: Freely while in active growth, but keep almost dry in winter

Feeding: Not necessary

Propagation: Division of offsets

Pests and diseases: Trouble free

Good companions: *Aloe* species, *Echeveria* species

aglaonema

Native to tropical forest floors of Asia, these rhizomatous perennials can survive in relatively shady conditions and are surprisingly resistant to temperature fluctuations. This makes them good foliage plants for offices and hallways

A. commutatum 'Pseudobracteatum'
Golden evergreen
The mid-green leaves are mottled with white and pale green.

A. crispum 'Marie'
This compact slow-growing plant has pronounced variegation.

A. 'Silver King'
The leaves are predominantly silver-grey in colour.

General care: Clean leaves occasionally. Repot every other year in spring. Cut back leggy plants to the base. Pinch out the small white flowers to encourage leaf growth.

Height and spread: 40cm (16in)

Temperature: Warm room, minimum 15°C (60°F)

Humidity: Tolerates dry air

Light: Bright indirect, but tolerates poor light

Watering: Moderately while in active growth. Keep compost just moist in winter

Feeding: Twice while in active growth

Propagation: Stem cuttings or division of rootball in spring

Pests and diseases: Mealy bugs

Good companions: *Dracaena fragrans*, *Maranta leuconeura*

Aglaonema crispum 'Marie'

aloe

Similar in appearance to agaves, these easily grown succulents enjoy the same dry, sunny conditions. *Aloe vera* is prized for its moisturising properties and often used as an ingredient in body lotions and shampoos. Increasingly available as a pot plant, it is suitable for the kitchen windowsill. Many people recommend *A. vera* for burns, stings or itches. Simply cut or break off a piece of leaf and squeeze the viscous sap onto the affected area to soothe it and initiate healing.

A. aristata Lace aloe
The small tight rosette of grey-green leaves is covered in tiny white spikes. Occasionally produces a spike of orange flowers.

A. variegata Partridge-breasted aloe
Overlapping V-shaped leaves form a tight rosette and are banded with white. A spike of orange-pink flowers may develop.

A. vera
This interesting plant is useful and easy to grow. In optimum growing conditions the loose rosette of very fleshy, grey-green, toothed leaves may produce a flower spike bearing dozens of tubular yellow flowers.

General care: May be moved outdoors during summer. Gently sponge the leaves occasionally to remove dust. A top-dressing of gravel will help to keep the neck of the plant dry.
Height and spread: 30cm (12in)
Temperature: Normal room, minimum 10°C (50°F)
Humidity: Dry air, but tolerates humid air
Light: Bright, including direct sun
Watering: Freely while in active growth, almost dry in winter
Feeding: Once or twice during the growing season
Propagation: Division of offsets
Pests and diseases: Will rot if over-watered
Good companions: *Agave* species, *Faucaria tigrina*

Aloe vera

anthurium

Striking, exotic 'flowers', borne intermittently throughout the year, are the main attraction of this large genus of evergreen perennials from the Americas. Each waxy flower is made up of a heart-shaped spathe and a prominent spadix. The spathe is usually red, although pink and white cultivars are also available. Individual flowers remain attractive for many weeks.

A. andraeanum Flamingo flower, Oilcloth flower
This is usually sold as red, pink or white cultivars. 'Red Angel' has large leaves and pinkish spathes. 'Red Love' has dark red spathes.

A. scherzerianum Flamingo flower, Pigtail plant
The brilliant red spathes have a contrasting yellow-to-white spadix. The many cultivars differ slightly in flower colour and size. 'Rothschildianum' has white spots on the spathe. 'Wardii' has large, dark red spathes.

Anthurium andraeanum cultivar

General care: Clean leaves regularly. Carefully pull off spent flowers. Repot every spring using a pot one size up; if the pot is too large, anthuriums produce foliage growth at the expense of flowers.
Height and spread: 40cm (16in)
Temperature: Warm room, minimum 15°C (60°F)
Humidity: Moderate, otherwise leaf tips go brown
Light: Bright but indirect

Watering: Moderately while in active growth in summer, sparingly in winter
Feeding: Monthly during the growing season, from spring until mid-autumn
Propagation: Division of rootball in spring
Pests and diseases: Mealy bugs, red spider mite
Good companions: *Monstera deliciosa*, *Philodendron* species

aphelandra

Only one species of this South American genus of evergreen shrubs and sub-shrubs is widely available as a houseplant. Grown for both its flowers and foliage, this small Brazilian shrub is usually offered for sale just as it comes into flower.

A. squarrosa Zebra plant

It is easy to see how this aphelandra came by its common name, as its leathery leaves sport pronounced white stripes. It is worth growing for the foliage alone, which is fortunate as repeat flowering can be difficult to induce. Individual blooms are short-lived, but the waxy yellow bracts from which they emerge remain decorative for many weeks. The most commonly grown cultivars are two compact plants, 'Dania' and 'Louisae'.

General care: Avoid low temperatures and over-watering, as these cause the lower leaves to drop. Clean the leaves regularly.
Height: 40cm (16in)
Spread: 30cm (12in)
Temperature: Warm room, minimum 15°C (60°F)
Humidity: Moderate to high
Light: Bright, including direct sun on all but the hottest summer days
Watering: Keep compost moist while in active growth, and just moist in winter
Feeding: Monthly in the growing season
Propagation: Stem cuttings
Pests and diseases: Trouble free
Good companions: *Anthurium* cultivars, *Streptocarpus* cultivars

Aphelandra squarrosa

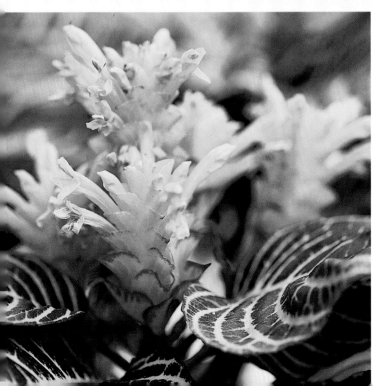

araucaria

The monkey-puzzle tree (*A. araucana*), which is sometimes seen in parks and gardens, is the best known member of this genus of tropical rainforest evergreen conifers. All are capable of growing up to 30m (100ft) in the wild, but the only species suitable for growing as a houseplant is unlikely to exceed 1.5m (5ft) indoors. Apart from bonsai, this is the only conifer houseplant.

A. heterophylla Norfolk Island pine

With branches growing in distinct tiers, young trees make attractive specimen houseplants. They grow best in a cool room and should never be placed near a radiator, as the warm dry air would turn the prickly needles brown.

General care: Grow in a soil-based compost and repot in spring, when the plant begins to look top-heavy. During summer stand the plant outdoors in a shady spot.
Height: 1.5m (5ft) **Spread:** 1m (3ft)
Temperature: Cool to normal room, not below 5°C (41°F)
Humidity: Not fussy in a cool room, but needs higher humidity in a warm room
Light: Bright but indirect
Watering: Freely while in active growth from spring to autumn but sparingly in winter; it will not recover if the roots dry out
Feeding: Monthly from spring to late summer
Propagation: Best to buy new plants
Pests and diseases: Trouble free
Good companions: *Plectranthus forsteri*, *Tolmiea menziesii*

Araucaria heterophylla

Graceful fern-like foliage is the main attraction of these South African perennials, which add contrast to mixed plant groups and flowering pot plants. They do best in a cool room and are not too fussy about humidity, as long as they are not in direct sun. If conditions suit, small white flowers are followed by berries.

A. densiflorus Sprengeri Group Asparagus fern

The feathery stems of this evergreen perennial look good on a shelf, or in a planter or basket. *A. densiflorus* 'Myersii' (foxtail fern) has closely packed, upright stems.

A. falcatus

This easy-care climber has curved leaves.

Asparagus falcatus

asparagus

A. setaceus (syn. A. plumosus) Asparagus fern

The delicate leaves of this climber are held in flat sprays. Beware of small sharp thorns on the climbing stems.

General care: Cut away yellowing stems near the base. Repot every spring.

Height and spread: 75cm (2½ft)

Temperature: Cool to normal. Keep clear of radiators

Humidity: Mist occasionally or group with other plants to increase local humidity

Light: Bright but indirect. Tolerates poor light levels.

Watering: Freely while in active growth in summer but do not allow the compost to become waterlogged. Moderately in winter

Feeding: Monthly in the growing season

Propagation: Division of rootball in spring

Pests and diseases: Trouble free

Good companions: *Asplenium nidus,* x *Fatshedera lizei*

aspidistra

These evergreen rhizomatous perennials really do thrive on neglect. They were popular foliage plants in Victorian times because of their resilience to coal fire and gas lamp fumes and tolerance of shade. Hardy enough to be grown outside in mild areas, they are a good choice for a north-facing room or cold stairwell or hallway.

A. elatior Cast-iron plant

The dark green leaves of this Chinese woodland native can be polished to a brilliant shine. Variegated cultivars need reasonable light if they are to maintain their markings: 'Milky Way' is speckled with yellow dots and 'Variegata' has creamy white streaks.

General care: Clean the leaves occasionally. Aspidistras like to be potbound so move to a bigger pot only when absolutely necessary.

Height: 60cm (2ft)

Spread: 30cm (1ft)

Temperature: Normal room

Humidity: Not fussy

Light: Best in indirect light, but tolerates darker conditions. Avoid direct summer sun

Watering: Moderately while in active growth. Keep just moist in winter

Feeding: Not essential but will benefit from an occasional liquid feed during the growing season

Propagation: Division of rootball in spring

Pests and diseases: Red spider mite, scale insects

Good companions: *Aglaonema* cultivars, *Fatsia japonica* cultivars

Aspidistra elatior

aucuba

Commonly used in the garden, these evergreen shrubs also make good foliage houseplants, especially for porches and hallways as they prefer cool rooms and can withstand a cold draught. They also tolerate erratic watering and low light levels, although variegated types do best in reasonable light; they will suffer if positioned near a radiator. The red berries that are sometimes produced outdoors on female plants do not develop indoors.

A. japonica Spotted laurel

Variegated cultivars of the glossy mid-green Japanese species make the most interesting plants. 'Crotonifolia' has yellow spots and speckles. The leaves of 'Picturata' have a large, central splash of yellow. 'Sulphurea Marginata' has yellow leaf margins and irregular yellow splashes. All parts may cause stomach ache if ingested.

Aucuba japonica 'Crotonifolia'

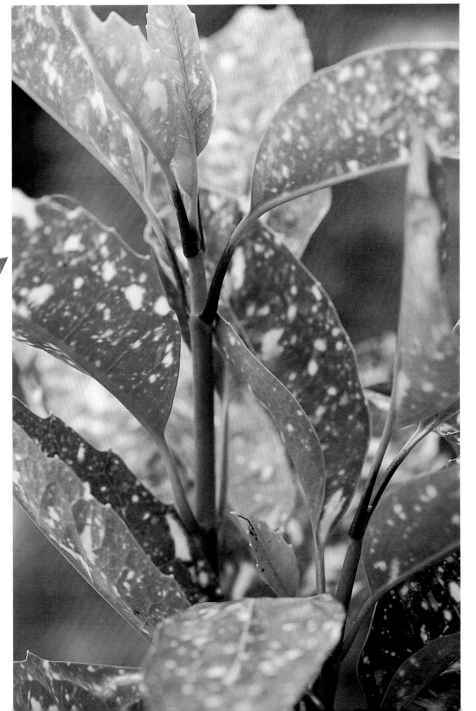

General care: Repot and prune to size in spring. Clean the leaves occasionally.

Height: 75cm (2½ft) **Spread:** 60cm (2ft)

Temperature: Cool room

Humidity: Tolerates dry air

Light: Poor to good

Watering: Freely while in active growth, sparingly in winter

Feeding: Monthly during the growing season

Propagation: Stem cuttings

Pests and diseases: Red spider mite

Good companions: *Cyclamen persicum* cultivars, *Fatsia japonica* cultivars

bromeliads

Despite their exotic looks, many bromeliads are fairly undemanding and so make good houseplants. Most can be left to their own devices for a couple of weeks, even over summer, without coming to any harm.

Most bromeliads are natives of tropical America, where they grow in trees (and are known as epiphytic bromeliads) or on the ground (terrestrial bromeliads). Tree-perching epiphytic species take moisture and nutrients from rainwater and plant debris that accumulate around their roots and in a 'vase' at the centre of their rosette. Some species of the bromeliad *Tillandsia* are air plants. They absorb airborne moisture and nutrients through tiny grey leaf scales, which give them a silvery appearance. In some bromeliads, the bracts form a striking and complex flower head held high above the foliage. In others, the flowers emerge from the centre of the 'vase', just above water level. Individual flowers are small and short-lived but the bracts remain decorative for months. Each rosette flowers once before it gradually dies.

General care: Bromeliads are best grown in free-draining compost of half by volume vermiculite and soil-less compost. They are inclined to rot in waterlogged conditions, especially where temperatures are low.

Temperature: Warm room, never below 13°C (55°F), but flowering is more likely to occur in a room at about 24°C (75°F)

Humidity: Not fussy except air plants, which require high humidity; mist them daily with soft water

Light: Bright light with some exposure to direct sun, except air plants, which may be scorched by direct summer sun

Watering: Use soft water (rainwater or water that has been boiled and allowed to cool) and pour directly into the 'vase' where present. Every few months change the water. In winter allow the 'vase' to drain completely before refilling

Feeding: Apply a liquid feed at half strength monthly between spring and late summer. 'Vase' plants need only a tiny drop of fertiliser

Propagation: Division of offsets

Pests and diseases: Trouble free unless planted deeply in compost that is over-watered. Mealy bugs and scale insects may be a problem.

Aechmea fasciata
Urn plant

Grown for its striking flower head, this epiphytic bromeliad forms a rosette of silvery grey leaves up to 60cm (2ft) across. Small purple flowers emerge from a spiky pink flower head. Give this plant plenty of room to grow, as brushing against it will damage the silvery bloom on the leaves. Also, the leaf edges are armed with tiny sharp spines.

Billbergia x windii

This clump-forming epiphytic species will spread over time to fill a pot. The spectacular red-bracted, greenish flowers are produced in summer. It is tolerant of temperatures as low as 10°C (50°F), but will flower only if it is in a sunny and warm position. After flowering, allow the plant to die back slightly before cutting the bloom off to make room for the offsets to grow.

Guzmania lingulata

Perhaps the most cultivated of all bromeliads, this epiphytic species is prized for its glossy leaves and spike of overlapping pale pink, orange or brilliant red or yellow bracts, which enclose yellow flowers. *G. conifera* has a cone-shaped flower head with yellow-tipped red bracts. In both species the bracts are extremely long-lasting.

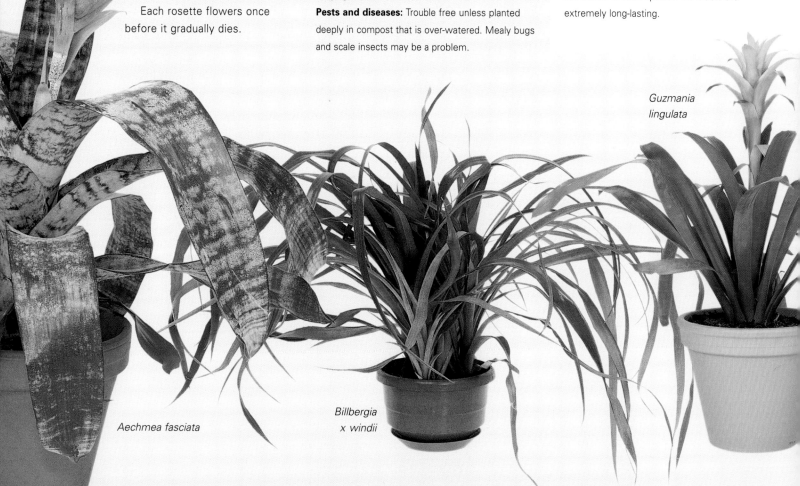

Guzmania lingulata

Aechmea fasciata

Billbergia x windii

Neoregelia carolinae 'Tricolor'
Blushing bromeliad

Commonly used in offices and shopping malls, this easy-care epiphytic bromeliad has leaves that are longitudinally striped with cream. When the plant flowers, the central 'vase' turns brilliant red.

Tillandsia cyanea

Large purple flowers emerge from the waxy pink bracts above the loose rosette of grass-like leaves. This epiphytic species, which is not an air plant, takes up moisture through its roots. Very different in appearance is spanish moss (*T. usneoides*), a grey tillandsia, or air plant, that takes in moisture through its tangled mass of small wiry leaves. It grows abundantly in the Florida everglades, where it hangs from tree branches.

Another air plant, *T. ionantha*, forms a small grass-like tuft from a bulbous base.

Vriesea splendens
Flaming sword

Like many vriesea species, this variable epiphytic or terrestrial bromeliad is grown for the dual attraction of its foliage and flower spikes. The leaves have broad purple-green bands and the tall sword-like flower spike comprises red bracts from which emerge the yellow flowers. *V. hieroglyphica* has irregular dark green marks on its foliage and a branched spike of yellowish flowers; it makes a large plant up to 1m (3ft). *V. carinata*, with a height and spread of 25cm (10in), produces flattened, waxy, red-and-yellow flower spikes.

Tillandsia cyanea

Neoregelia carolinae 'Tricolor'

Vriesea splendens

begonia

Native to tropical and sub-tropical regions, this vast and varied genus includes many good foliage or flowering houseplants.

B. x corallina 'Lucerna'
Cane-stemmed begonia
This easy-care begonia is grown for both its large, asymmetric green leaves, which are speckled silver on top and ruby-red below, and occasional clusters of pale pink flowers. Generous feeding and watering produces luxuriant growth.

B. Elatior hybrids
Although their natural season is winter, numerous hybrids are available all year, as they come into flower in white, yellow, pink, orange or red, some with deeply cut petals. All are compact and bushy, with succulent stems and glossy leaves.

General care: Deadhead regularly. Cut down cane-stem tops if they become too tall and use as cane cuttings; repot every spring.
Height: 30–60cm (1–2ft)
Spread: 30–50cm (12–20in)
Temperature: Normal room, minimum 10ºC (50ºF) for cane-stemmed plants
Humidity: Not fussy
Light: Indirect
Watering: Freely during active growth, moderately in winter
Feeding: Monthly for cane-stemmed begonias during active growth. Not necessary for Elatior hybrids
Propagation: Check garden centre or nursery label for plant type. Cane-stemmed: cuttings or division. Buy new plants for Elatior hybrids
Pests and diseases: Trouble free
Good companions: *Chlorophytum comosum, Schefflera arboricola*

Begonia
Elatior hybrid

Calathea makoyana

calathea

Most of these evergreen perennials from tropical forests are grown for their boldly variegated and purple-suffused foliage.

C. crocata
The orange-red waxy flower heads develop in summer and are long-lasting. The plain leaves are ruby underneath.

C. lancifolia Rattlesnake plant
This has long lance-shaped, pale green leaves with darker patches and red-purple undersides.

C. makoyana Cathedral windows
Light shines through the heavily patterned leaves, giving rise to the common name.

C. roseopicta 'Rosastar'
The pale green leaves are edged with dark green and have red undersides.

C. sanderiana
This forms a compact clump of striped cream-and-green foliage.

C. zebrina
Brown stripes spread out from the midrib of the velvety leaves.

General care: Clean leaves occasionally. Repot every spring.
Height: 45cm (18in) **Spread:** 30cm (12in)
Temperature: Warm room, not below 15ºC (60ºF)
Humidity: High. Mist daily. Stand on a tray of dampened pebbles
Light: Poor to good. Direct summer sun will burn the leaves
Watering: Keep moist while in active growth but water only moderately in winter
Feeding: Two or three times while in active growth
Propagation: Division of rootball
Pests and diseases: Red spider mite
Good companions: *Ctenanthe* species, *Maranta* species, *Stromanthe* species

calceolaria

Pouch flower, Slipper flower

Slipper flowers come from a range of habitats in Central and South America. Those most widely available for use as flowering pot plants are the Herbeohybrida Group. As well as supplying temporary colour in the home, they are also often used in outdoor summer bedding schemes.

C. Herbeohybrida Group

The strange inflated blooms of these compact biennials come in bright shades of red, orange and yellow, and are often speckled. Modern cultivars are so floriferous that the crinkled foliage is almost totally obscured. Available in flower from late spring to midsummer; the blooms last for about one month.

C. integrifolia 'Sunset'

Held in branching spikes above the foliage, the inflated bronze-red pouches appear in midsummer.

General care: Discard plants when flowering is over. When buying, look for specimens with lots of buds.

Height: 45cm (18in) **Spread:** 20cm (8in)

Temperature: Normal room

Humidity: Not fussy

Light: Bright but indirect

Watering: Keep compost moist

Feeding: Not necessary

Propagation: Easiest to buy new plants; can be raised from seed in a greenhouse

Pests and diseases: Trouble free

Good companions: *Begonia* Elatior hybrids, *Exacum affine*

Calceolaria integrifolia 'Sunset'

campanula

Bellflower

Numerous popular garden plants, nearly all with bell-shaped, blue flowers, belong to this large genus. One species lends itself particularly well to indoor cultivation, but is only noteworthy when in flower.

C. isophylla

Falling stars, Italian bellflower

Throughout summer the semi-trailing stems of this perennial are covered in a mass of blue starry flowers. It can be bought as a pot plant as it is coming into flower and either discarded in autumn, when the blooms are over, or cut back and overwintered in a cool room. 'Alba' has white flowers. 'Flore Pleno' has double flowers.

General care: Deadhead to prolong flowering.

Height: 15cm (8in)

Spread: 30cm (12in)

Temperature: Flowering is prolonged in a cool room

Humidity: Not fussy

Light: Bright but indirect

Watering: Keep compost moist while flowering, but just moist if overwintering

Feeding: Every 2–3 weeks while flowering

Propagation: Stem cuttings root easily in water

Pests and diseases: Trouble free

Good companions: *Calceolaria* Herbeohybrida Group, *Primula obconica* cultivars

Campanula isophylla

As a houseplant, this compact annual is usually available in late summer to autumn, as the fruits ripen from green through yellow to red. It makes a cheerful if temporary addition to a sunny windowsill, providing as much interest as any flowering plant, and with the bonus of being useful for cooking. Juice from the fruits can, however, cause a burning sensation on the skin.

C. annuum cultivars Chilli pepper, Paprika

The dwarf cultivars of the naturally tall species are widely available as pot plants. The decorative fruits are either conical or spherical and should last for 2–3 months.

General care: Discard plants once they are past their best.

Height and spread: 20cm (8in)

Temperature: Warm room but away from radiators; hot dry air causes the fruit to fall

Humidity: Fairly high. Mist plants daily or stand on dampened pebbles

Light: Bright, including direct sun

Watering: Keep compost moist

Feeding: Not necessary

Propagation: Seed or buy new plants

Pests and diseases: Red spider mite

Good companions: Chrysanthemum cultivars, Cyclamen persicum culitvars

Capsicum annuum cultivar

capsicum

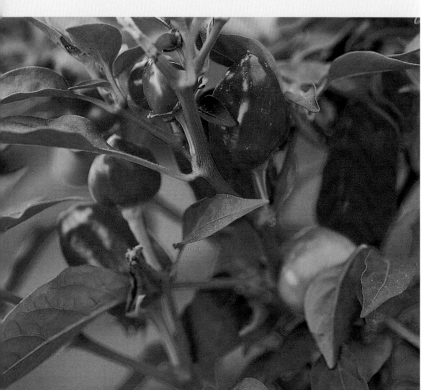

catharanthus

Only one species in this small genus is grown as a houseplant. In its native Madagascar it is an evergreen perennial, but as a flowering pot plant it is best treated as an annual and discarded in the autumn when it stops flowering in response to falling light levels. Chemicals found in this plant are artificially synthesised for the production of drugs to fight childhood leukemia.

C. roseus Madagascar periwinkle

Provided there is enough light, the cerise-pink flowers are borne all through summer. 'Albus' is a white-flowered cultivar, while the blooms of plants in the Ocellatus Group have a contrasting red eye. All parts of the plant may cause discomfort if ingested.

General care: Pinch out shoots to promote bushiness.

Height and spread: 30cm (12in)

Temperature: Normal room

Humidity: Mist daily, when not in direct sun or the petals may be marked

Light: Bright, including direct sun

Watering: Keep moist

Feeding: Monthly

Propagation: Seed in spring

Good companions: Hibiscus rosa-sinensis, Impatiens New Guinea Group

Catharanthus roseus

ceropegia

Only one species in this diverse genus of some 200 species is suitable for growing as a houseplant.

C. linearis subsp. woodii
Hearts-on-a-string, Rosary vine
This slightly succulent plant makes an interesting and low-maintenance specimen plant for a hanging basket. It is grown primarily for its trailing habit and marbled leaves, which are coloured purple on the underside. In good light it will also produce tubular mauve flowers in late summer and autumn. Small tubers produced in the leaf joints can be detached and potted up to create new plants. Underground offset tubers also can be separated to form new plants. Ceropegia is prone to rot in wet conditions so water sparingly at all times.

General care: The fragile stems make repotting difficult so try to replace the top layer of compost every spring. Top-dress with gravel to keep the crown dry. Prune back straggly shoots.
Trailing height: 1m (3ft) **Spread:** 20cm (8in)
Temperature: Warm room, but tolerates temperatures down to 5°C (41°F) when not in active growth
Light: Moderate to bright
Humidity: Does best in dry air
Watering: Sparingly when in active growth. Keep almost dry in winter
Feeding: Once or twice with a dilute liquid feed when in active growth
Propagation: Root or stem tubers. Pot these up into cactus compost, placing them just below the surface
Pests and diseases: Trouble free
Good companions: *Faucaria* species, *Sedum morganianum*

Ceropegia linearis subsp. *woodii*

chlorophytum

Represented in cultivation by *C. comosum* and its variegated cultivars, this genus of southern and western African evergreen rhizomatous perennials grows new plantlets at the end of arching stems. These are easily detached and potted up to produce new plants.

C. comosum Spider plant
The green-leaved species is tolerant of a wide range of conditions, except cold and bright sunlight, which bleaches the leaves. Its variegated cultivars are more popular: 'Variegatum' has creamy white leaf margins; 'Vittatum' has a white band down the centre; while 'Bonnie' has twisted leaves. The arching leaves and stems are best displayed by growing plants in a hanging basket. Research has shown that in a small room a single specimen removes 98 per cent of the carbon monoxide in the air.

General care: Pull off dead leaves. Repot every spring.
Height: 40cm (16in) **Spread:** 50cm (20in)
Temperature: Normal room
Humidity: Tolerates dry air, although this tends to make the leaf tips go brown
Light: Bright but indirect
Watering: Freely during active growth in spring and summer, but moderately at other times
Feeding: Twice while in active growth
Propagation: Plantlets
Pests and diseases: Trouble free
Good companions: *Dracaena marginata*, x *Fatshedera lizei*

Chlorophytum comosum 'Vittatum'

chrysanthemum

Chrysanthemum cultivar

Cheap and cheerful, pot 'mums' are excellent for bringing temporary colour into the home. They are undemanding and need to be watered only occasionally, yet provide weeks of blooms. After flowering, either discard or plant in the garden. If they transplant successfully they will grow to over 1m (3ft) in height (they are treated with dwarfing hormones in the nursery) and flower the following autumn. This humble pot plant has been shown to be one of the best species for absorbing the common household toxin formaldehyde from the air (see page 115).

Chrysanthemum cultivars

There is a vast array of cultivars available and new types are constantly being developed, but plants are usually just sold under the generic name of 'chrysanthemum'. Flower heads come in different shapes and sizes: some are single and daisy-like, others double, and there are pompons, too. They are available in every colour except blue. Buy a plant where the buds are just beginning to open; check inside the plant's plastic cover to make sure there is no grey mould on the foliage.

General care: Snip off spent flowers.

Height and spread: 25cm (10in)

Temperature: Normal room, but flowering is prolonged in a cool room

Humidity: Not fussy

Light: Not fussy

Watering: Keep compost moist

Feeding: Not necessary

Propagation: Buy new plants

Pest and diseases: Prone to grey mould, especially if kept too long in a plastic wrapper

Good companions: *Begonia* Elatior hybrids, *Exacum affine*

cissus

Several robust and vigorous climbing vines of this tropical genus make excellent foliage houseplants. They can be grown in hanging baskets or tall planters as trailing plants. To grow them as climbers, provide support, such as wires or trellis, for the tendrils to cling to.

C. antarctica Kangaroo vine
This vine has large, shiny, toothed leaves, and can grow to more than 2m (6ft).

C. discolor
The heart-shaped leaves are marked with silver and the undersides are red.

C. rhombifolia Grape ivy
This long-lived resilient plant will grow rapidly, so position it where it has room to expand. The dark green, toothed leaves have reddish hairs beneath.

General care: Repot or top-dress every spring. Plants that are outgrowing their space can be cut back hard in spring.

Height and spread: 2m (6ft)

Temperature: Normal room

Humidity: Not fussy

Light: Not fussy, except for *C. discolor*, which needs bright indirect light to maintain good leaf variegation. Very bright sun will scorch the leaves

Watering: Moderately while in active growth, sparingly in winter. Better slightly on the dry side rather than constantly wet at the roots

Feeding: Occasionally in growing season

Propagation: Stem cuttings or simple layering

Pests and diseases: Red spider mite

Good companions: *Aspidistra elatior*, *Peperomia* species

Cissus rhombifolia

Clivia miniata

clivia

These South African evergreen perennials must be kept cool and almost dry over winter to initiate flowering in spring. Alternatively, start with a new plant every spring. Look for plants where the flower spike is just visible amongst the leaves.

C. miniata Kaffir lily

This commonly grown foliage houseplant produces long strap-like leaves that grow up from the fleshy bulb-like base. The single flower spike pushes up from the centre, and in early spring the buds open to large orange-red flowers that last for several weeks. Occasionally, there is a second flowering in late summer. 'Aurea' has yellow flowers.

General care: Cut off the dead flower spike at its base. Repot only when the roots push the plant out of its pot.

Height and spread: 45cm (18in)

Temperature: Normal room from flowering to late autumn, then cool room to rest, minimum 10°C (50°F)

Humidity: Not fussy

Light: Bright but indirect

Watering: From when the flower buds form until late autumn, keep the compost moist then water just enough to prevent the compost drying out

Feeding: Once as the flower spike begins to elongate and 2–3 times through the summer

Propagation: Division of offsets

Pests and diseases: Trouble free

Good companions: Best grown alone

codiaeum

Grown for their brightly coloured foliage, these Pacific Island shrubs provide year-round interest. In the wild they may reach 2m (6ft), but the cultivars grown as houseplants are unlikely to exceed half of that size. Insignificant white flowers are sometimes produced, but these should be pinched out to encourage the growth of more leaves. Plenty of light and steady warmth are necessary to keep the leaf colour bright.

C. variegatum var. pictum
Joseph's coat

The oval or lobed leathery leaves are marked with green, yellow and red. Dozens of cultivars, varying in shape, size and coloration, are available. 'Sunrise', for example, has long slender leaves with yellow midribs. The oval leaves of aptly named 'Commotion' are a riot of green, purple, pink, yellow and red.

General care: Clean the leaves regularly. Top-dress or repot in spring.

Height: 1m (3ft) **Spread:** 60cm (2ft)

Temperature: Warm room, not below 15°C (60°F). Draughts and wide temperature fluctuations cause leaf drop

Humidity: Prefers humid air

Light: Bright, including direct sun on all but the hottest summer days

Watering: Freely while in active growth, moderately in winter. Downward-pointing leaves are a sign that the plant needs watering. Avoid getting water on the leaves as this will mark them

Feeding: Monthly while in active growth, from spring to autumn

Propagation: Stem cuttings

Pests and diseases: Mealy bugs, red spider mite, scale insects

Good companions: *Anthurium* cultivars, *Aphelandra* cultivars

Codiaeum variegatum var. pictum

columnea

Goldfish plant

Several evergreen trailing shrubs and sub-shrubs of this American genus make good specimens for a tall planter or shelf. All have pairs of opposite leaves and bear flamboyant tubular flowers in spring; all plants mentioned here bear scarlet blooms streaked with yellow. Although these are rainforest plants, they resent being too wet and will quickly rot if the compost is waterlogged for any length of time.

C. x banksii

In a warm and bright position, this shiny-leaved species will bear flowers all year.

C. microphylla

This sub-shrub has hairy flowers and leaves covered with reddish hairs. 'Variegata' has white-margined grey-green leaves.

C. schiedeana

Pinch out shoots regularly to keep this quick-growing plant compact.

General care: Trim back over-long stems after flowering. Repot or top-dress every spring.

Height: 2m (6ft) **Spread:** 20cm (8in)

Temperature: Normal room, minimum 10°C (50°F)

Humidity: High

Light: Bright but indirect

Watering: Moderately while in active growth. Keep compost almost dry over winter

Feeding: Two or three times while in active growth

Propagation: Stem cuttings

Pests and diseases: Aphids, mealy bugs

Good companions: *Guzmania* cultivars, *Solenostemon* cultivars

Columnea x *banksii*

cordyline

Two cordyline species make good houseplants. In the wild they would both become trees, but do not attain these dimensions in the home. These are fairly tough undemanding plants that can be long-lived where conditions suit them.

C. australis Cabbage tree

Long slender leaves and a slow-growing trunk make this an architectural plant that lends itself to modern interiors. It is also a garden plant and good for containers. Purpurea Group has dark purple-brown leaves. 'Red Star' has pinkish red leaves. 'Torbay Dazzler' has cream-margined leaves and is tolerant of direct sun; it benefits from being moved outside in summer.

C. fruticosa (syn. C. terminalis)

Good luck plant, Tea or ti tree

This evergreen shrub has strap-shaped, deep green leaves. Over time it develops a somewhat spindly trunk, which is best dealt with by cutting out the top 20cm (8in) and using this as a cutting to make a new plant. The leaves of 'Kiwi' are striped yellow and green and have pink edges. 'Baby Ti' is a dwarf cultivar with bronze leaf edges.

General care: Cut or pull off dead leaves. Repot every spring.

Height: 1.5m (5ft) **Spread:** 1m (3ft)

Temperature: Normal room, minimum 10°C (50°F)

Humidity: *C. australis* is not fussy; *C. fruticosa* prefers moderate to high humidity

Light: Bright

Watering: Freely while in active growth, sparingly at other times

Feeding: Monthly while in active growth

Propagation: Cane cuttings

Pests and diseases: Red spider mite, scale insects

Good companions: *Begonia* x *corallina* 'Lucerna', *Gynura aurantiaca*

Cordyline australis 'Torbay Dazzler'

crassula

Several plants in this large genus of African and Asian succulent perennials and shrubs make good low-maintenance specimens for a sunny windowsill. They are able to conserve water in their fleshy stems and leaves, but should be watered quite freely during the summer growing season. As they are inclined to become top-heavy with age, grow them in terracotta or stone pots for extra stability.

C. arborescens Silver dollar plant
The fleshy leaves of this succulent shrub are matt grey. Mature plants produce clusters of small pink flowers in late summer and autumn.

C. ovata Jade tree, Money tree
This is similar in appearance to *C. arborescens* but its glossy, mid-green oval leaves are sometimes edged with red, and it bears small white flowers in late summer and autumn. 'Hobbit' has peculiar rolled-together leaves.

General care: Prune to shape in spring. Repot or top-dress every other year in spring. Plants may be stood outside in summer.
Height and spread: 1m (3ft)
Temperature: Normal room, not below 10°C (50°F)
Humidity: Tolerates dry air
Light: Bright, including direct light
Watering: Keep compost moist while in active growth in summer. Water just enough in winter to prevent it drying out completely
Feeding: Once or twice while in active growth
Propagation: Stem cuttings or leaf stalk cuttings
Pests and diseases: Mealy bugs
Good companions: *Aloe* species, *Echeveria* species

Crassula ovata

ctenanthe

Native to the damp forest floors of Brazil and Costa Rica, these evergreen perennials require fairly high humidity to thrive. Given the right conditions, they make striking foliage houseplants.

C. lubbersiana
The large leathery leaves are heavily marked with yellow blotches. The tall stems may need to be staked.

C. oppenheimiana
The upper surface of the leaves is beautifully marked with green and silver, and the underside is bright pink. 'Tricolor' (never-never plant) has creamy white variegation with pale and dark green, and intermittent spikes of white flowers.

C. setosa 'Compactstar'
Dark green, herringbone-pattern leaves; red on the underside.

General care: Keep the leaves clean. Repot every spring.
Height: 1m (3ft) **Spread:** 50cm (20in)
Temperature: Warm room, minimum 15°C (60°F)
Humidity: High; dry air causes the leaf margins to go brown
Light: Indirect, avoiding summer sun
Watering: Moderately while in active growth, sparingly in winter
Feeding: Two or three times while in active growth
Propagation: Division of rootball in spring
Pests and diseases: Trouble free
Good companions: *Calathea* species, *Maranta leuconeura*

Ctenanthe lubbersiana

cycas

Cycad, Sago palm

A fascinating group of palm-like plants, cycads have been around since the age of the dinosaurs. They are grown for their handsome rosettes of stiff needle-like leaves, which emerge from a squat rounded trunk. In the wild the trunk slowly elongates into a 2m (6ft) tree. Pot-grown specimens are much smaller and unlikely to produce more than a couple of new leaves per year. Cycads are covered by CITES (Convention on Trade In Endangered Species) so buy only nursery-raised plants.

C. revoluta Japanese sago palm

As this slow-growing plant is one of the most expensive houseplants available, be sure you can give it the conditions it needs – plenty of light and warmth, combined with careful watering.

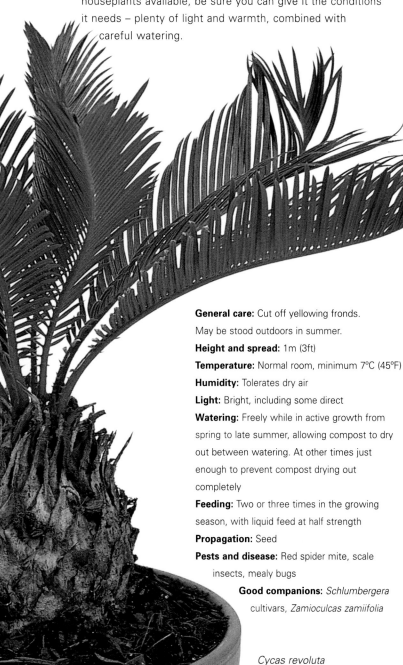

General care: Cut off yellowing fronds. May be stood outdoors in summer.

Height and spread: 1m (3ft)

Temperature: Normal room, minimum 7°C (45°F)

Humidity: Tolerates dry air

Light: Bright, including some direct

Watering: Freely while in active growth from spring to late summer, allowing compost to dry out between watering. At other times just enough to prevent compost drying out completely

Feeding: Two or three times in the growing season, with liquid feed at half strength

Propagation: Seed

Pests and disease: Red spider mite, scale insects, mealy bugs

Good companions: *Schlumbergera* cultivars, *Zamioculcas zamiifolia*

Cycas revoluta

cyclamen

When situated in a cool room, cyclamens provide a good display for several months. Flowers may be pink, red or purple, but the pure white best shows off the silver marbling in the leaves. After flowering, the corm can be allowed to dry out for a period of dormancy over summer, and then repotted and brought into growth again in the autumn. Alternatively, buy a fresh plant; look for lots of buds hidden within the foliage.

C. persicum Florists' cyclamen

There is a vast array of cultivars available, including some with scented flowers and also unusual types with frilly or serrated petals, but the precise name is not usually specified on the label. The main period for florists' cyclamen is autumn to spring.

General care: Pull off spent flowers and yellowing leaves where they meet the corm.

Height and spread: 20cm (8in)

Temperature: Cool room

Humidity: Not fussy in a cool room, but mist frequently in a warm one

Light: Bright but indirect

Watering: Keep compost just moist, watering at the base of the plant

Feeding: Not necessary

Propagation: Seed or buy new plants

Pests and disease: Grey mould and rot if over-watered

Good companions: *Fatsia japonica* cultivars, *Rhododendron simsii* cultivars

Cyclamen persicum cultivar

Cyclamen persicum cultivar

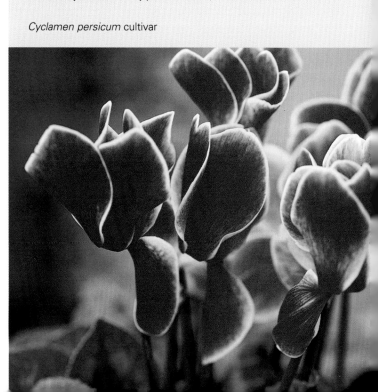

cyperus

Usually associated with boggy ground, this large genus of rush-like plants occurs in tropical and sub-tropical areas throughout the world. The most famous member of this genus is papyrus, or egyptian paper rush (*C. papyrus*), which is a very vigorous plant. More suitable for the home are the following species of cyperus, which are good for people who tend to over-water houseplants.

C. albostriatus 'Variegatus'

Similar to *C. involucratus*, but in this case the stems and leaves are decoratively striped in white.

C. involucratus (syn. C. alternifolius)

Umbrella plant

This elegant architectural plant is grown for its attractive foliage, but it also bears small grass-like flowers throughout summer. 'Nanus' is a dwarf variety.

General care: Divide congested clumps to increase vigour. Use a soil-based compost when repotting. Cut off brown leaves close to the base.

Height: 60cm (2ft) **Spread:** 30cm (12in)

Temperature: Normal room, minimum 10°C (50°F)

Humidity: Moderate to high. Dry air causes the leaf tips to go brown

Light: Bright but indirect

Watering: Freely at all times

Feeding: Monthly while in active growth

Pests and diseases: Trouble free

Propagation: Stem cuttings (especially when inverted in a jar of water – a shoot will develop from the submerged tip) or division of rootball

Good companions: Best grown on its own

Cyperus involucratus

dieffenbachia

Dumb cane

Grown for their handsome leaves and lush appearance, dumb canes make good single specimens but also associate well with other plants. Native to tropical forest floors of the Americas, these evergreen perennials enjoy humid conditions and indirect light; dry air and direct sun will damage the leaves. All parts of the plant are toxic, so take care when propagating or pruning.

D. seguine (syn. D. maculata, D. picta)

The large glossy leaves of this upright, single-stemmed plant are speckled with white. Numerous cultivars have been developed: 'Amoena' is particularly robust and has yellowish green markings around the leaf veins; 'Camille' has pale yellow-green leaves with dark green edges; and the leaves of 'Exotica' are heavily splashed with white. 'Reflector' has irregular pale green markings on the leaves.

Dieffenbachia seguine 'Reflector'

General care: Keep the leaves clean. Over time the plant will develop a bare trunk, which can be cut back to a 15cm (6in) stump and should re-sprout.

Height: 1m (3ft) **Spread:** 50cm (20in)

Temperature: Warm room, minimum 15°C (60°F).

Humidity: High

Light: Indirect

Watering: Keep compost moist when in active growth, in spring and summer, and just moist at other times

Feeding: Monthly when in active growth

Propagation: Stem cuttings

Pests and diseases: Mealy bugs

Good companions: *Aglaonema* cultivars, *Philodendron* cultivars

dionaea

Venus fly trap

This single species genus is a rosette-forming perennial that is native to the bogs of both North and South Carolina, USA. It is fascinating because of its ability to catch and 'eat' insects as a means of supplementing its nutrient intake.

D. muscipula

Although it is not an easy plant to grow, it is worth trying as a curiosity – children are particularly enthralled by its gruesome eating habits. The hinged leaves are fringed with spines and on the surface there are also three small hairs, known as the trigger hairs. When a fly touches the trigger hairs, the leaf snaps shut in just a third of a second. The victim is then squeezed betwen the lobes while the plant absorbs the nutrients from its body. The plant is prone to die suddenly if humidity and watering regimes do not suit it. The surface colour of the leaves is a guide as to the well-being of the plant – the deeper the red the healthier it is, and flaccid green lobes are a bad sign.

Dionaea muscipula

General care: Snip off dead 'traps' with scissors.

Height: 10cm (4in) **Spread:** 8cm (3in)

Temperature: Normal room

Humidity: Moderate to high. Mist daily

Light: Bright, including direct sun

Watering: Keep compost moist at all times by standing pot in a saucer of soft water

Feeding: Not necessary

Propagation: Division of rootball in spring

Pests and diseases: Trouble free

Good companions: *Cyperus involucratus*

dracaena

As these evergreen shrubs and trees from tropical Africa mature, the lower leaves fall away to reveal a slender trunk with a crown of arching linear leaves, which may be striped with white, cream or red. Dracaenas make good specimen plants, especially where height is needed. Those described here tolerate a wide range of conditions, including erratic watering, and can be long-lived. The plants within this genus have been renamed several times, and labels are not always correct.

D. fragrans 'Lemon Lime'

This glossy-leaved cultivar has bright lime green-and-yellow stripes, while the dark green leaves of 'Warneckei' are striped white. 'Massangeana' has broad leaves with lime-green stripes. 'Janet Craig' produces extremely dark green foliage and is good for absorbing the common household toxin formaldehyde from the air (see page 115). The last two mentioned cultivars are frequently listed under *D. glauca*.

D. marginata

The elegant narrow leaves of this virtually indestructible plant have red edges. 'Tricolor' has cream and red stripes.

D. reflexa 'Song of India'

This freely branching plant has broad yellow leaf edges. 'Song of Jamaica' has dark green leaves with a light green central stripe.

General care: Clean leaves occasionally. Pull away yellowing leaves. If plants get too tall, cut them back – they will sprout from lower down the stem. Use the cuttings for propagation.

Height: 2m (6ft) **Spread:** 1m (3ft)

Temperature: Warm room, minimum 15°C (60°F)

Humidity: Tolerates dry air

Light: Indirect, but tolerates low light levels if kept almost dry

Watering: Freely while in active growth from spring to autumn. Keep compost just moist at other times

Feeding: Monthly while in active growth

Propagation: Cane cuttings

Pests and diseases: Mealy bugs, scale insects

Good companions: *Ficus benjamina*, *Howea fosteriana*

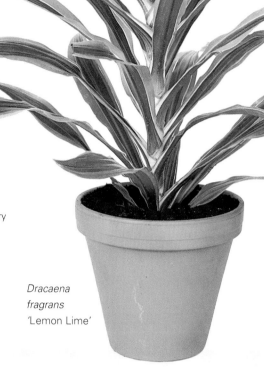

Dracaena fragrans 'Lemon Lime'

echeveria

Native to dry and semi-desert areas from the southern USA to the Andes, these rosette-forming succulents have attractive, green, purple or blue, fleshy leaves. Dainty, yellow-and-pink flowers are produced on tall flower spikes in summer. Echeverias make neat, low-maintenance indoor specimens for a sunny spot and associate well with other succulents and cacti. The whitish bloom on some leaves is easily marked if they are handled.

E. agavoides

Resembling an agave, this species has sharply pointed, triangular leaves, tipped with red.

E. elegans

The plump, silvery blue leaves are arranged in a tight rosette.

E. 'Perle von Nürnberg'

The fleshy purple leaves are held in a flat rosette.

General care: Ensure good ventilation around the plant and if possible stand outside for a while in summer. A top-dressing of gravel will help to keep the neck of the plant dry.

Height and spread: 8cm (3in)

Temperature: Normal room. Tolerates temperatures down to almost freezing as long as the compost is dry

Humidity: Prefers dry air

Light: As much light as possible

Watering: Moderately while in active growth, very sparingly at other times

Feeding: Two or three times from spring to summer

Pests and diseases: Vine weevil grubs may get into the compost of plants positioned outdoors for the summer

Propagation: Stalked leaf cuttings

Good companions: *Aloe* species, *Crassula* species

Echeveria 'Perle von Nürnberg'

echinopsis

The cacti in this large South American genus range in shape from small and spherical to tall and columnar. They are tough plants, only likely to suffer if over-watered. Many species will grow in shaded conditions and tolerate temperatures down to almost freezing point, provided the compost is dry and the plants are not too sappy. They flower freely, producing large blooms in a range of colours.

E. chamaecereus   Peanut cactus
This forms a dense mass of creeping cylindrical stems and bears scarlet flowers in summer. It needs less sun than *E. eyriesii*.

E. eyriesii
Sporting almost black spines, this cactus ages from a globular to a cylindrical shape. In summer, its scented, white, 20cm (8in) long flowers, being moth pollinated, open late in the day.

General care: Repot when 2cm (¾in) from the edge of the container, using cactus compost. Beware of the spines; protect your hands by holding the plant in a paper collar (see page 141).

Height: 25cm (10in) **Spread:** 10cm (4in)

Temperature: Normal room but tolerates a cool room

Echinopsis species

Humidity: Does best in dry air

Light: Bright but indirect for best growth

Watering: Sparingly at all times, keeping compost almost dry over winter, especially if not in much light

Feeding: Monthly from spring to late summer

Propagation: Division of offsets

Pests and diseases: Mealy bugs

Good companions: *Faucaria* species, *Opuntia* species

eichhornia

Water hyacinth

A single species of this South American genus of floating plants is widely available. Sold through aquatic centres for outdoor ponds, it can be grown indoors in a bowl of water to make an unusual temporary display. Grow it in a glass container to show off the long purple roots.

E. crassipes
The glossy leaves are attached to inflated stems, which make the plant buoyant. In summer dense spikes of pale blue, funnel-shaped flowers are produced.

General care: Float plants in a container of soft water (rainwater, or water that has been boiled and allowed to cool). Remove yellowing leaves as well as spent flowers promptly.

Height and spread: 15cm (6in)

Temperature: Normal room, minimum 10°C (50°F)

Humidity: Moderate to high

Light: Bright but filtered is best

Watering: Not necessary

Feeding: Not necessary

Propagation: Best to buy new plants in spring

Pests and diseases: Trouble free

Good companions: Best grown alone

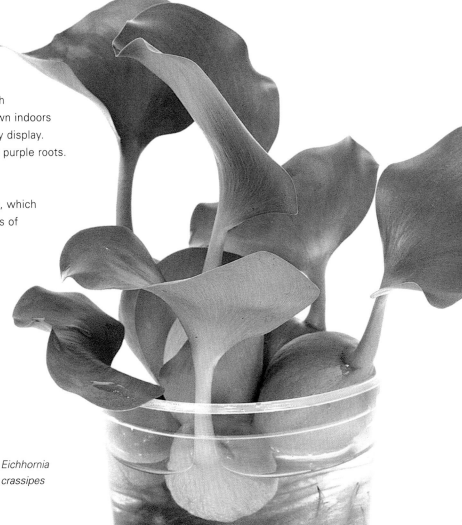

Eichhornia crassipes

Belonging to a small group of climbers from south-east Asia and the western Pacific, epipremnums can be grown up a moss pole or cascading down from a basket or tall planter. Root nodules form along the stem, making propagation very easy. Only one species is widely available.

E. aureum (syn. Scindapsus aureus) Devil's ivy

Even though it is native to the forests of the Solomon Islands, devil's ivy prefers a bright spot. Mature leaves are streaked with yellow, but if the light is poor new ones are nearly all green. Poor light also causes leaves to be small. The white variegation of 'Marble Queen' is also best in good light. 'Neon' has bright yellowish green leaves and tends to be short-lived.

Epipremnum aureum 'Marble Queen'

epipremnum

General care: Dust or sponge leaves occasionally. If plant gets too big or leggy, cut back to initiate new growth from lower down the stem. Repot every spring.

Height and spread: Indefinite

Temperature: Normal room

Humidity: Tolerates dry air

Light: Bright but no direct sun in summer

Watering: Freely while in active growth, sparingly in winter

Feeding: Monthly between spring and late summer

Propagation: Air layering or stem cuttings

Pests and diseases: Trouble free

Good companions: *Codiaeum* cultivars, *Monstera deliciosa*

episcia

Flame violet

These South American creeping and trailing perennials are grown for their pretty puckered leaves and brightly coloured flowers, which are produced intermittently throughout summer. Episcias need high humidity to thrive.

E. cupreata

The silvery green leaves have brownish markings around the edges and purple undersides. The orange-red, tubular flowers have a yellow eye. There are many hybrids to choose from: 'Tropical Topaz', for instance, has pale green foliage and yellow flowers.

E. dianthiflora

This species has soft-haired, dark green leaves and bears white flowers with finely fringed petals.

E. reptans

The brownish green leaves are veined with silver, and the flowers are red.

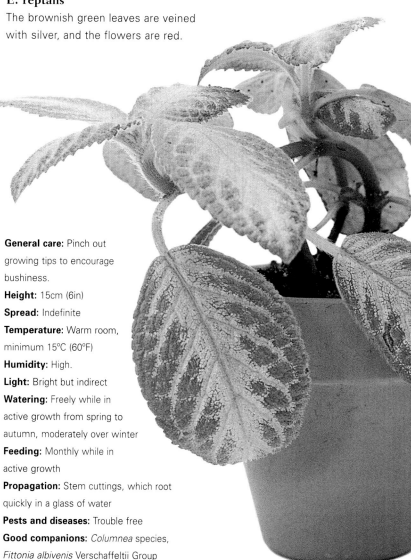

General care: Pinch out growing tips to encourage bushiness.

Height: 15cm (6in)

Spread: Indefinite

Temperature: Warm room, minimum 15°C (60°F)

Humidity: High.

Light: Bright but indirect

Watering: Freely while in active growth from spring to autumn, moderately over winter

Feeding: Monthly while in active growth

Propagation: Stem cuttings, which root quickly in a glass of water

Pests and diseases: Trouble free

Good companions: *Columnea* species, *Fittonia albivenis* Verschaffeltii Group

Episcia cupreata

euonymus

Many species of this large genus of shrubs, trees and climbers are grown in gardens, but young plants of *E. japonicus* and *E. fortunei* and their cultivars make good foliage specimens for cold porches and stairwells. They can be pruned hard to keep them compact and bushy.

E. fortunei

This tough little shrub has dark green leaves but the variegated cultivars are more commonly seen. Cheerful 'Emerald 'n' Gold' is the most popular, both indoors and in the garden.

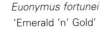

E. japonicus

Japanese spindle

When grown in the garden this glossy evergreen shrub may reach 3m (10ft), but it can be kept small by pruning its branches and restricting its roots in a pot. Variegated cultivars make the most interesting specimens.

General care: Prune to size in spring. Repot every spring using soil-based compost.

Height and spread: 60cm (2ft)

Temperature: Cold to cool room

Humidity: Not fussy

Light: Green varieties tolerate low light levels but variegated types need bright light including some direct sun

Watering: Freely while in active growth, sparingly in winter

Feeding: Monthly from spring to late summer

Propagation: Stem cuttings

Pests and diseases: Red spider mite

Good companions: *Aucuba japonica* cultivars, *Hedera* species

Euonymus fortunei
'Emerald 'n' Gold'

euphorbia

Euphorbia is a huge and diverse genus containing trees, shrubs, perennials, annuals and succulents. The flowers themselves are insignificant but are surrounded by large colourful leaf-like or petal-like bracts. The milky sap secreted when the plant is damaged may irritate the skin.

E. milii Crown of thorns

This woody, thorny stemmed shrub is easy to grow and requires very little maintenance. In a brightly lit spot it will bear its red flowers almost all year round.

E. pulcherrima Poinsettia

Sold exclusively just before Christmas, this plant has brilliant red, leaf-like bracts. Various cultivars are available, some with cream or pink bracts. Team it with green-leaved plants to show off the bracts, or group it with white florists' cyclamen and ivy for a festive display.

E. trigona

Resembling an upright, branching cactus, this succulent has triangular stems armed with spines. It is grown for its architectural interest and is unlikely to flower in the home. Although it can survive without much water, if watered and fed regularly throughout the summer it will put on an impressive growth spurt.

General care: Poinsettias must be protected from cold and draughts; unless well wrapped, even the journey from the shop to the car on a cold winter's day can be enough to damage a plant fatally. They are best discarded once they are past their best. *E. milii* and *E. trigona* should be top-dressed with gravel.

Height and spread: 45cm (18in)

Temperature: Minimum 15°C (60°F)

Humidity: Tolerates normal conditions

Light: Bright

Watering: Keep poinsettias moist. Water *E. milii* and *E. trigona* sparingly

Feeding: Not necessary

Propagation: Best to buy new poinsettia plants. Stem cuttings: *E. milii* and *E. trigona*

Pests and diseases: Trouble free

Good companions: *Begonia* Elatior hybrids, *Chrysanthemum* cultivars

Euphorbia milii

exacum

Persian violet

Just one of the 25 species in this Middle Eastern genus is widely available as a flowering pot plant. It is offered for sale in the summer months.

E. affine

Even though this compact evergreen perennial is best discarded once the freely flowering blooms are over, it is well worth buying for its sweet scent alone. The mauve-blue, five-petalled flowers have bright yellow stamens and last over a long season. 'White Midget' has white flowers.

General care: Deadhead to prolong flowering.

Height and spread: 25cm (10in)

Temperature: Normal room

Humidity: Ideally moderate to high, although plants tolerate dry air

Light: Bright, indirect sun

Exacum affine 'White Midget'

Watering: Keep compost moist

Feeding: Not necessary

Propagation: Sow seed in spring or buy plants with plenty of buds

Pests and diseases: Trouble free

Good companions: *Begonia* Elatior hybrids, *Kalanchoe blossfeldiana* cultivars

x fatshedera

The single plant in this hybrid genus is derived from *Fatsia japonica* and *Hedera* (ivy). It is trailing in habit but as it does not produce the aerial roots that enable ivy to climb, it needs either to be tied into canes or to have the shoots pinched out to keep it bushy.

x F. lizei Tree ivy

The glossy, dark green leaves of this evergreen shrub are deeply lobed. It tolerates low light levels and low temperatures almost down to freezing, so is useful for poorly lit hallways. The variegated forms are more appealing but a little more exacting in their requirements, needing reasonable light and warmth: 'Annemieke' has yellow-marked leaves; and 'Variegata' has white marks.

General care: Keep the foliage clean. Repot every spring.

Height: 1m (3ft) **Spread:** 50cm (20in)

Temperature: Cool room for the species, warm room for its cultivars

Humidity: Not fussy when temperatures are low, but needs higher humidity in warm rooms

Light: Bright but indirect

Watering: Moderately at all times, but sparingly if plants are exposed to cold conditions

Feeding: Two or three times while in active growth

Propagation: Stem cuttings

Pests and diseases: Red spider mite

Good companions: *Aspidistra elatior, Aucuba japonica* cultivars

x *Fatshedera lizei* 'Annemieke'

fatsia

Aralia

Prized for its handsome shiny leaves, *F. japonica* is the most widely grown member of this tiny genus. It is often seen growing in gardens where it can become a sizeable shrub and produces spherical heads of white flowers in autumn.

F. japonica

Grown indoors, this vigorous evergreen shrub makes a good specimen foliage plant that is unlikely to exceed 1m (3ft) and does not develop flowers. The deeply cut leaves are up to 30cm (12in) across. Hardy and tolerant of low light levels, it is a good choice for a cool and draughty hallway or stairwell. 'Variegata' has cream leaf tips and edges and is a less vigorous plant.

General care: May be stood outside in a shady spot in frost-free months. Prune to size in spring.

Height and spread: 1m (3ft)

Temperature: Cool to normal room

Humidity: Not too fussy, but does better if occasionally misted or grouped with other plants to raise local humidity, especially if the room gets hot

Light: Poor to good but avoid direct summer sun

Watering: Moderately while in active growth, sparingly at other times. Drooping leaves are a sign the plant needs watering

Feeding: Monthly from spring to late summer

Propagation: Seed or stem cuttings

Pests and diseases: Red spider mite, especially in dry air

Good companions: *Aspidistra elatior, Aucuba japonica* cultivars

Fatsia japonica

Faucaria tigrina

faucaria

Tiger jaws

The fleshy triangular leaves of this South African genus of succulents are edged with soft spines, which resemble teeth in an open jaw. Native to semi-desert areas, faucarias need only scant watering; over-watering plants in winter especially will quickly make them rot. When grown in correct light levels, they produce daisy-like flowers in late summer and autumn. It may be necessary to source plants from a cacti and succulent nursery.

F. tigrina

Where conditions suit it, this yellow-flowered plant produces offsets around it.

F. tuberculosa

This is similar to *F. tigrina*, but the leaves are studded with small white dots.

General care: Divide and repot when the clump is 2cm (¾in) from the edge of the pot, using cactus compost.

Height: 10cm (4in) **Spread:** 20cm (8in)

Temperature: Cool room, minimum 5°C (41°F)

Humidity: Prefers dry air

Light: As much as possible

Watering: Sparingly while the plant is receiving lots of summer sun, at other times keep compost almost dry. Avoid getting water on the leaves

Feeding: Once or twice in summer

Propagation: Division of rootball in spring

Pests and diseases: Mealy bugs

Good companions: *Ceropegia linearis* subsp. *woodii, Lithops karasmontana* subsp. *bella*

ferocactus

Aptly named (Latin *ferox* means 'fierce'), these cacti have ferocious spines – usually hard and curved at the tips like fishhooks. They are easy to grow and make intriguing additions to a cactus collection, but need to be handled with the protection of a paper collar (see page 140).

F. latispinus

This ridged globular native of Mexico bears pink and brown spines. In summer, pink to purple, white or yellow flowers may be produced on mature plants.

General care: Repot when the body of the cactus is 2cm (¾in) from the edge of its pot, using cactus compost.

Height and spread: 15cm (6in)

Temperature: Normal room

Humidity: Tolerates dry air

Light: Bright, including direct sun

Watering: Sparingly while in active growth in summer, but allow compost to dry out between watering. Keep almost dry in winter

Feeding: Monthly from spring to late summer, applying a liquid feed at half strength

Propagation: Seed, but easier to buy new plants

Pests and diseases: Mealy bugs

Good companions: *Lithops* species, *Mammillaria* species

Ferocactus latispinus

ficus

Fig

Some of the best foliage houseplants are to be found in the large fig genus . Their stature adds impact to displays and they make good focal points or single specimens. In the wild these trees can grow to 30m (100ft), but are unlikely to exceed 2.5m (8ft) in the home. They are not especially fast growing so if a tall plant is required it is best to buy one. They are also good for absorbing common airborne toxins, especially formaldehyde (see page 115).

F. benghalensis 'Audrey'

This evergreen tree often produces horizontal branches and usually bears large, single-stemmed, papery, matt green leaves.

F. benjamina Weeping fig

This evergreen small tree or shrub has gently arching branches and glossy oval leaves. It is the easiest fig to care for. 'Starlight' has leaves marked heavily with white, but is less vigorous. 'Golden Monique' has lime-green variegation and wavy leaf edges.

F. elastica 'Robusta'
Rubber plant

Could be mistaken for *F. benghalensis* but for its rubbery dark green leaves, which can be polished to a brilliant shine. The foliage of 'Doescheri' is mottled with dark and light green and white. 'Petit Melany' is a densely branching dwarf cultivar with dark purple-green leaves.

General care: Clean leaves occasionally. Young plants may need the support of a cane. Prune to size in spring, bearing in mind the milky sap may irritate the skin.

Height: 2.5m (8ft) **Spread:** 1.5m (5ft)

Temperature: Normal room, minimum 10°C (50°F).

Humidity: Not fussy

Light: Bright but avoid direct summer sun. Variegated cultivars need most light

Watering: Thoroughly when in active growth, then allow compost to become fairly dry before watering again. In winter keep just moist

Feeding: Monthly from spring to late summer

Propagation: Stem cuttings. *F. elastica*: air layering

Pests and diseases: Mealy bugs, red spider mite, scale insects

Good companions: *Dracaena fragrans* 'Warneckei', *Nolina recurvata*

Ficus benjamina

ferns

Prized for their graceful fronds, ferns work well as single specimens or planted in a group. Their arching habit and soft shapes also add harmony to a collection of plants.

Although they are found in a range of habitats and belong to a number of different plant families, ferns are unified by their primitive method of reproduction and existed long before flowering plants evolved. They develop tiny dust-like spores, which are held in small brown cases (sori) on the undersides of their fronds. Most ferns grow in moist, humid, shady environments, so in the home the bathroom may be the best place for them. *Asplenium nidis* and *Blechnum gibbum* are the largest, reaching 1m (3ft) in height. Most others grow to about 30cm (12in) in height and spread.

General care: Cut off older yellowing fronds as near to the base as possible.

Temperature: Warm room, minimum 15°C (60°F), except for asplenium and nephrolepis, which prefer minimum 10°C (50°F), and adiantum, which prefers minimum 7°C (45°F)

Humidity: High. Group plants on dampened pebbles and mist daily. Ferns with thicker leaves, such as pellaea, are more tolerant than those with very fine fronds, such as adiantum.

Light: Bright but indirect light. Direct sun will burn the fronds

Watering: Keep compost permanently moist but do not allow to stand in water

Feeding: Monthly between spring and autumn using a liquid feed at half strength

Propagation: Spores, but this is difficult. Division of rootball for rhizomatous ferns, such as adiantum and pteris, in spring

Pests and diseases: Mealy bugs, scale insects

Adiantum raddianum
Maidenhair fern

Native to tropical areas of North and South America, this beautiful plant has very exacting requirements, as its fine fronds are particularly sensitive to dry air and direct sun. When older fronds start to deteriorate, snip the black stalks off as near to the crown as possible.

Asplenium nidis
Bird's nest fern

The common name refers to the open rosette formed by the shiny leaves as well as to its habit of growing on tree branches. The fronds, which are entire rather than divided, slowly unfurl from the centre of the rosette. This fern tolerates poor light levels.

Blechnum gibbum
Miniature tree fern

Over time this Fijian fern develops a short trunk, from the top of which unfurls a rosette of deeply cut fronds. It is fairly tolerant of dry air.

Adiantum raddianum

Asplenium nidis

Blechnum gibbum

Nephrolepis exaltata

This plant spreads by sending out stolons (running stems) across the surface of the compost, at the end of which develop new plantlets. It is excellent for removing the common household toxin formaldehyde from the air (see page 115). The most popular cultivar is Boston fern ('Bostoniensis'), which forms a dense clump of deeply divided, arching fronds and is good for a hanging basket.

Tolerates poor light levels but does better in brighter but indirect light. 'Teddy Junior' is small.

Pellaea rotundifolia
Button fern

Although this New Zealand and Australian native occurs in dry regions, it should never be allowed to dry out at the roots. The low, arching fronds bear thick, almost circular leaflets. It makes a good underplant for larger pots, as it will send out its rhizomes to produce new clumps.

Pteris cretica

Cretan brake fern The fronds of this neat and elegant fern comprise slender leaflets. The popular var. *albolineata* has a white stripe down the centre of each leaflet. 'Cristata' leaflets are crested.

Nephrolepis exaltata

Pellaea rotundifolia

Pteris cretica

fittonia

Native to tropical rainforests of Peru, these highly decorative low-growing evergreen foliage plants require warmth and high humidity for success, so a position in the kitchen or bathroom may suit them. If you place the pot on damp pebbles to increase local humidity, ensure that it is not standing in water, as fittonias will not thrive in sodden compost. The occasional insignificant white flowers are best pinched out.

F. albivenis Argyroneura Group
Silver net leaf
The bright green oval leaves of this compact plant have pronounced white veins.

F. albivenis Verschaffeltii Group
Painted net leaf
The olive-coloured leaves have bright pink veins.

General care: Pinch out shoots to promote bushiness.
Height: 10cm (4in) **Spread:** Indefinite
Temperature: Warm room, mimimum 15°C (60°F)
Humidity: High. Mist plants daily to prevent leaf edges going brown. Stand pot on a tray of dampened pebbles
Light: Semi-shaded

Watering: Moderately at all times
Feeding: Monthly from spring to summer
Propagation: Cuttings, layering
Pests and diseases: Trouble free
Good companions: *Aphelandra squarrosa, Hypoestes phyllostachya*

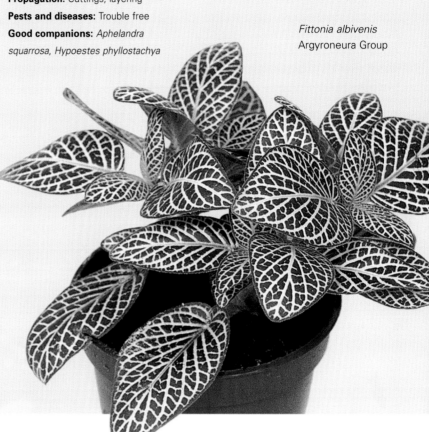

Fittonia albivenis
Argyroneura Group

gardenia

A large genus of evergreen shrubs and trees from tropical regions of Asia and Africa, gardenias have showy scented flowers. By far the most commonly cultivated houseplant species is *G. jasminoides*.

G. jasminoides (syn. G. augusta)
Cape gardenia, Common gardenia
This stocky glossy-leaved native of Japan and China is renowned for its intensely fragrant white flowers produced in late spring and summer. It is a fairly easy plant to grow in the short term, but needs constant warmth if it is to flower in subsequent years. Widely fluctuating temperatures prevent flower buds from forming, or cause any that have formed to fall.

General care: Remove flowers once they begin to turn brown. Prune to shape after flowering has finished. Repot every spring using ericaceous (lime-free) compost.
Height and spread: 60cm (2ft)
Temperature: Normal room, minimum 10°C (50°F)
Humidity: High. Stand pots on trays of dampened pebbles
Light: Bright, including direct sun
Watering: Keep compost moist at all times, using soft water
Feeding: Monthly from spring to late summer
Propagation: Cuttings
Pests and diseases: Mealy bug, red spider mite
Good companions: *Codiaeum* cultivars, *Solenostemon* cultivars

Gardenia jasminoides

gerbera

As brightly coloured pot plants, these hairy-leaved perennials provide a longer-lasting display than as cut flowers. If you buy a plant just as it is coming into bloom, it should flower for a couple of months. Plants are available throughout summer, and are best discarded once they have finished flowering.

Gerbera jamesonii cultivar

G. jamesonii cultivars Transvaal daisy

Dozens of cultivars of this South African species are available with single or double daisy-like flowers in a range of colours. They make stockier plants than the species, and the flowers are held on shorter stems. These plants are excellent for absorbing formaldehyde from the air.

General care: Remove yellowing leaves and spent flowers promptly.
Height: 30cm (12in) **Spread:** 25cm (10in)
Temperature: Normal room
Humidity: Not fussy
Light: Bright but indirect
Watering: Keep compost moist
Feeding: Once or twice over summer, using a tomato fertiliser
Propagation: Sow seed in spring or autumn, or buy new plants
Pests and diseases: Trouble free
Good companions: *Begonia* Elatior hybrids, *Chrysanthemum* cultivars

gynura

Of the 50-plus species in this genus of scrambling evergreen sub-shrubs and perennials from tropical areas of Africa and Asia, only one species is sufficiently decorative to be a houseplant.

G. aurantiaca
Purple velvet plant, Velvet plant

It is almost impossible not to stroke this plant when you see it, as the deep green leaves are densely felted with purple hairs. It has an erect, then scrambling habit, but may be either tied in to vertical supports or pinched out to keep it bushy. Small orange-yellow, dandelion-like flowers may emerge in spring.

General care: If plants get leggy, prune them back hard in spring. Repot every spring.
Height: 60cm (2ft)
Spread: 40cm (16in), if given support
Temperature: Normal room, minimum 10°C (50°F)

Humidity: High. Stand pots on trays of dampened pebbles
Light: Bright but indirect
Water: Moderately when in active growth, sparingly in winter
Feeding: Monthly throughout the growing season
Propagation: Cuttings
Pests and diseases: Red spider mite
Good companions: *Anthurium* cultivars, *Calathea* species

Gynura aurantiaca

haworthia

Many species of this genus of South African succulents, which grow as stemless rosettes, resemble aloes and enjoy similar conditions – lots of light and moderate watering. Haworthias can be very variable and may look quite different depending on conditions. For example, a generously watered plant in a sunny position will develop particularly fat, fleshy leaves, while one allowed to dry out in the sun may turn temporarily red. Most species form clumps by producing offsets.

H. attenuata
Although very variable, this always has fleshy triangular leaves covered in raised white bumps. In summer a tall flower spike bearing numerous white tubular flowers may develop.

H. cymbiformis
The densely packed fleshy leaves grow equally well in sun or indirect light.

H. venosa subsp. tessellata (syn. H. tessellata)
The plump, grey-green leaves of this cluster-forming plant carry pale net-like markings.

General care: Repot every other year in spring using cactus compost.
Height and spread: 12cm (5in)
Temperature: Cool room, minimum 5°C (41°F)
Light: As much as possible
Humidity: Likes dry air
Watering: Freely while in active growth, sparingly at other times
Feeding: Once or twice while in active growth
Propagation: Division of offsets
Pests and diseases: Mealy bugs
Good companions: Aloe species, Echeveria species

Haworthia attenuata

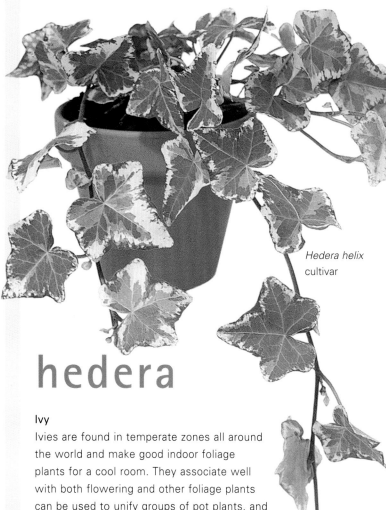

Hedera helix cultivar

hedera

Ivy

Ivies are found in temperate zones all around the world and make good indoor foliage plants for a cool room. They associate well with both flowering and other foliage plants can be used to unify groups of pot plants, and also clean the air. They can be grown up moss poles or trellis or can trail down from baskets. Their hardiness makes them useful for unheated porches and stairwells, and the non-variegated types grow where light levels are poor.

H. helix cultivars
The species itself is rarely grown as its numerous cultivars have more decorative leaves: 'Goldchild' has yellow edges; 'Oro di Bogliasco' has a pale yellow central splash; 'Glacier' has grey-green and white marks; and 'Eva' has white-edged leaves.

General care: Ivies are often sold in small pots and usually benefit from being potted on as soon as you get them home. Cut back over-long shoots as necessary.
Trailing height and spread: 1.5m (5ft)
Temperature: Cool or even cold room
Humidity: Not fussy if temperatures are low, but needs high humidity in a warm room
Light: Bright but indirect is best. Variegated types need more light than all-green ones
Watering: Keep compost just damp at all times
Feeding: Monthly from spring to late summer
Propagation: Stem cuttings or simple layering
Pests and diseases: Red spider mite, especially in dry conditions
Good companions: *Aspidistra elatior, Fatsia japonica*

heliotropium

Heliotropium arborescens 'Chatsworth'

Heliotrope
The approximately 250 heliotrope species are primarily native to sunny dry regions of the Americas. Cultivars of *H. arborescens*, often seen in summer bedding schemes, are the most commonly grown indoors for their intensely sweet scent.

H. arborescens Cherry pie
The perfumed purple flowers of the species are carried in large domed clusters. Cultivars are compact and free flowering: 'Chatsworth' is a reliable cultivar with very fragrant flowers; 'Marine' has dark purple flowers; the deep violet-blue blooms of 'Princess Marina' are particularly fragrant; and 'White Lady' is white flowered. These short-lived shrubs can be cut back and overwintered, but as plants tend to become leggy many people prefer to replace them each year.

General care: After flowering, either discard or cut back and overwinter in a cool room. Pinch out tips of young plants to promote bushiness and cut off faded flower heads.
Height: 30cm (12in) **Spread:** 25cm (10in)
Temperature: Cool to normal room, minimum 5°C (41°F)
Humidity: Stand on dampened pebbles

Light: Bright, including direct sun
Watering: Freely while in active growth. Keep compost just moist over winter
Feeding: Monthly from spring to late summer
Propagation: Stem cuttings
Pests and diseases: Trouble free
Good companions: *Campanula isophylla*, *Pelargonium* species

hibiscus

Most of the 200-plus species in this genus are tropical shrubs. They are grown for their exotic flowers, which are individually short-lived but produced over a long period. Hibiscus are greedy plants and respond well to regular watering and feeding from spring to late summer.

H. rosa-sinensis Rose of China
The large summer and autumn flowers of this vigorous evergreen shrub are usually red, but many cultivars are available, some with double flowers, in shades of red, orange, pink, yellow and white. Some have white variegation in the leaves, for example 'Cooperi'. Dry compost and/or low temperatures are likely to cause flower buds to be dropped. Mature specimens in large containers may grow much larger than indicated here.

General care: Cut plants back to a good framework in spring, and shorten over-long shoots as necessary. Repot every spring.
Height and spread: 1m (3ft)
Temperature: Normal room. Day and night temperatures should not fluctuate greatly
Humidity: Not fussy
Light: Bright, indirect sun

Watering: Freely between spring and late summer. At other times keep compost moist but not sodden
Feeding: Fortnightly from spring to late summer
Propagation: Stem cuttings
Pests and diseases: Aphids
Good companions: *Abutilon* hybrids, *Cordyline australis*

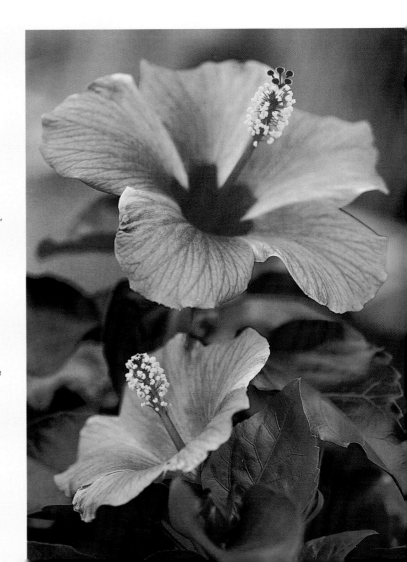

Hibiscus rosa-sinensis cultivar

hippeastrum

Often confused with amaryllis, hippeastrums are bulbous plants from Central and South America, with large strap-shaped, basal leaves that are produced with, or just after, the flowers. It is the huge-flowered hybrids that are often grown as houseplants, and in autumn, garden centres and supermarkets sell hippeastrum 'kits' containing all you need to grow these spectacular white, orange, pink or red winter flowers.

H. hybrids

Each bulb produces a stout flower stalk, which bears as many as six funnel-shaped flowers in colours that range from red, pink and orange to white, some with contrasting stripes on the petals. Large bulbs may produce two flower stalks. 'Apple Blossom' has pink-streaked white flowers, 'Christmas Gift' has pure white flowers, and 'Red Lion' has velvety deep red petals.

Hippeastrum
'Red Lion'

General care: Cut off the flower spike when the flowers fade. Pull away the withered leaves at the end of summer. Bulbs require a rest period after flowering.
Height: 45cm (18in) **Spread:** 30cm (12in)
Temperature: Normal room, except for the rest period from late summer to late autumn when pots need to be in a cool room
Humidity: Not fussy
Light: Bright
Watering: Keep compost moist from the time when bulbs are planted until late summer; during the rest period keep compost almost dry. Resume watering in late autumn

Feeding: Monthly while watering
Propagation: Division of offsets, but for best results buy new bulbs
Pests and diseases: Trouble free
Good companions: Usually grown on their own

hoya

Wax flower
Two species of this large genus of evergreen climbing and trailing plants can be grown indoors. They bear clusters of often highly scented, waxy flowers in summer, their fragrance being most powerful in the evening. Hoyas like humid conditions so might be best grown in the bathroom or kitchen.

H. carnosa Wax plant
This is essentially a larger version of *H. lanceolata* subsp. *bella*. It may grow to 3m (10ft) and is best trained as a climber tied into a support such as trellis. 'Variegata' has creamy white leaf edges.

H. lanceolata subsp. bella
(syn. H. bella)
Miniature wax plant
Originating from Burma, this trailing epiphyte (tree-perching plant) lends itself to cultivation in a hanging basket or tall planter. Such a container also provides the best view of the downward-facing, scented flowers. These are white with a red eye and appear during summer.

General care: Top-dress with fresh potting compost every spring.
Height and spread: 40cm (16in)
Temperature: Normal room, minimum 10°C (50°F)
Humidity: Moderate to high
Light: Bright, including direct sun
Watering: Keep the compost moist while the plant is in active growth, but water sparingly in winter, allowing the compost to become almost dry between watering
Feeding: Monthly while in active growth, from spring to late summer
Propagation: Stem cuttings
Pests and diseases: Trouble free
Good companions: *Catharanthus roseus*, *Musa* species

Hoya lanceolata
subsp. *bella*

hyacinthus

Hyacinth

Hyacinths introduce a welcome splash of colour and fragrance in the depths of winter. Specially prepared bulbs are available in late summer and autumn for indoor flowering between early winter and late spring, depending on the planting time. Plant several in bulb fibre with the 'nose' just showing or place a single bulb in a hyacinth glass with the base just touching the water. Place in a cool dark place for six weeks, until the shoot is 2cm (¾in) tall, then move to a bright spot indoors. Contact with the bulbs may cause skin irritation.

H. orientalis

There are dozens of cultivars, with flowers in white, yellow, apricot, pink, red and blue: 'L'Innocence' is white, 'City of Haarlem' yellow, 'Ostara' blue and 'Pink Pearl' pink.

General care: May be planted out in the garden after flowering, but cannot be used indoors again.
Height: 20cm (8in)
Spread: 10cm (4in)
Temperature: Normal room once shoot emerges, although flowering is prolonged in a cool room
Humidity: Not fussy
Light: Bright
Water: Keep compost moist or water level topped up
Feeding: Not necessary
Propagation: Buy fresh bulbs
Pests and diseases: Trouble free
Good companions: Normally grown on their own

*Hyacinthus
orientalis
'Ostara'*

hypoestes

Just one species of this genus of shrubby evergreen perennials from southern Africa and south-east Asia is cultivated as a houseplant, and occasionally as a summer bedding plant.

H. phyllostachya Freckle face, Polka dot plant

This little sub-shrub is grown for its heavily pink-speckled leaves. It produces spikes of rather insignificant flowers, but these should be pinched out, to encourage more leaf growth. Several cultivars are available, including red-speckled 'Carmina', and 'Wit', which has white-marbled leaves.

General care: Pinch out shoots regularly to promote bushiness. When the plant becomes leggy after a year or so, take cuttings and discard the parent plant.
Height and spread: 25cm (10in)
Temperature: Normal room, minimum 10°C (50°F)
Humidity: High
Light: Bright, including direct sun, for the best colouring
Watering: Keep compost moist at all times
Feeding: Monthly from spring to late summer
Propagation: Seed or stem cuttings
Pests and diseases: Trouble free
Good companions: *Fittonia albivenis, Gynura aurantiaca*

*Hypoestes
phyllostachya*

impatiens

Busy lizzie

The most widely grown examples of this large genus of tender annuals and perennials are *I. walleriana* and its cultivars, which are more commonly known as the summer bedding busy lizzies. Although these types can be grown indoors, they quickly become leggy. The closely related New Guinea Group make better indoor specimens and have slightly larger flowers over a long season.

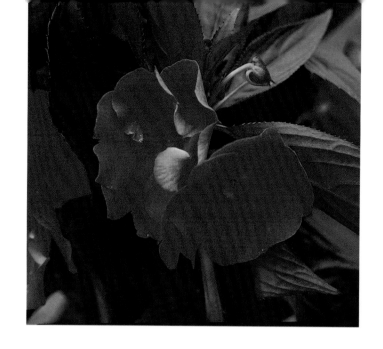

I. New Guinea Group

These juicy-stemmed perennials bear characteristic spurred impatiens flowers in a range of vivid colours that includes red, pink, orange and white. Various seed selections have been developed and the foliage may be green, dark purple or variegated with a central yellow blotch.

Impatiens New Guinea Group

General care: Deadhead to prolong flowering. Pinch out tips of young plants to promote bushiness. If plants become leggy, take cuttings and discard the parent plant.

Height: 30cm (12in) **Spread:** 20cm (8in)

Temperature: Normal room

Humidity: High

Light: Bright but indirect

Watering: Keep compost just damp at all times

Feeding: Every 2–3 weeks from spring to late summer

Propagation: Seed or stem cuttings

Pests and disease: Red spider mite

Good companions: *Calathea* species, *Heliotropium arborescens* cultivars

iresine

There are about 80 species of evergreen iresines, which come from dry areas of South America and Australia, but it is the cultivars of *I. herbstii* that are usually grown indoors. These are among the most brightly coloured of foliage plants and are easy to grow.

I. herbstii Beefsteak plant, Bloodleaf

This upright plant has succulent red stems and red leaves. 'Aureoreticulata' has green leaves with yellow veins. 'Brilliantissima' has purple leaves with pink veins.

General care: Pinch out shoots regularly to keep plant bushy. If plants become too leggy, take cuttings (which root easily in water) and discard the parent. Pot 3–5 cuttings in a single pot to create a stockier specimen.

Height: 45cm (18in) **Spread:** 30cm (12in)

Temperature: Normal room, minimum 10°C (50°F)

Humidity: Not fussy, but if the room is very warm, high humidity will prevent leaf tips going brown

Light: Bright, including direct sun, for best leaf colour

Watering: Freely during active growth. Keep compost of overwintered plants just moist

Feeding: Monthly from spring to late summer

Propagation: Stem cuttings

Pests and diseases: Aphids, red spider mite

Good companions: *Codiaeum variegatum* var. *pictum*, *Justicia brandegeeana*

Iresine herbstii 'Brilliantissima'

Jasmine

The jasmines grown as houseplants are twining climbers prized for their fragrant flowers. These vigorous plants quickly outgrow the wire hoop supports they are sold on so need to be provided with stronger ones, such as trellis. They are suited to conservatories, although their fragrance is so sweet it is worth buying a young flowering plant for temporary display elsewhere.

J. officinale

This fast-growing climber is usually semi-deciduous indoors, losing some leaves over winter. Very fragrant, white, star-shaped blooms are borne in summer.

Jasminum polyanthum

jasminum

J. polyanthum

Similar to *J. officinale* but is evergreen, pink-budded and winter flowering.

General care: Prune back after flowering. Repot or top-dress every spring. Snip off faded flower clusters.

Height: 3m (10ft) **Spread:** 1.5m (5ft)

Temperature: Cool to normal room

Humidity: Not fussy

Light: Bright but indirect

Watering: Freely while in active growth, sparingly at other times

Feeding: Monthly from spring to late summer

Propagation: Stem cuttings

Pests and diseases: Aphids, mealy bugs

Good companions: *Cissus discolor*, *Pelargonium* species

justicia

Most plants in this large genus of mainly tropical evergreen shrubs need humid conditions to thrive, but a couple of small flowering species are content with conditions in the home.

J. brandegeeana Shrimp plant

The common name of this Mexican shrub refers to the pinkish bracts that surround the small white flowers. These bracts bear a passing resemblance to cooked prawns, hence their nickname. Flowers throughout the summer. 'Yellow Queen' has yellow bracts.

J. rizzinii

In winter this small rounded shrub bears tubular flowers that are flushed with red and yellow.

Justicia brandegeeana

General care: Pinch out shoots to promote bushiness. Straggly plants can be pruned fairly hard in spring.

Height and spread: 45cm (18in)

Temperature: Normal room

Humidity: Not fussy, but in a very warm room stand on a tray of dampened pebbles

Light: Bright light, including direct sun

Watering: Moderately

Feeding: Monthly from spring to late summer

Propagation: Stem cuttings

Pests and diseases: Trouble free

Good companions: *Abutilon* hybrids, *Iresine herbstii*

kalanchoe

Widespread in tropical and semi-desert regions, this large and diverse genus ranges from annuals to trees. The most widely grown kalanchoes are small succulents, prized primarily for their long-lasting brightly coloured flowers, although in some species silvery felted leaves are the main attraction. All are easily grown plants for a sunny windowsill.

K. blossfeldiana hybrids Flaming Katy
Available in bloom at any time of the year, these bushy perennial succulents bear tight clusters of white, yellow, pink or red flowers above softly toothed, fleshy leaves. Plants can be kept once flowering is over, but they tend to become rather leggy.

K. fedtschenkoi 'Variegata'
White-variegated, blue-green leaves are the attraction of this trailing shrubby succulent, which produces roots along its stems.

Kalanchoe blossfeldiana hybrid

K. manginii
This semi-trailing plant bears clusters of red tubular flowers.

K. thyrsiflora
This foliage plant has red-edged, pale green, fleshy leaves joined in pairs at the bases, and bears fragrant yellow flowers.

General care: Pinch out faded flowers.

Height and spread: 30cm (12in)

Temperature: Normal room

Humidity: Tolerates dry air

Light: Bright, including direct sun

Watering: Keep compost just moist

Feeding: Not necessary for *K. blossfeldiana* hybrids, but other species benefit from feeding during spring and summer

Propagation: Division of offsets or plantlets, or stem cuttings

Pests and diseases: Trouble free

Good companions: *Crassula* species, *Echeveria* species

Lithops species

lithops

Living stones
Originating in stony semi-desert areas of South Africa, these little succulent perennials resemble the pebbles they grow amongst. In late summer daisy-like, yellow or white flowers may emerge from between the pair of mottled, flat-topped, fat leaves. Lithops are fairly easy to grow provided they get a lot of sun and very little water. There are about 40 species, all essentially quite similar except for variations in the leaf colouring.

L. karasmontana subsp. bella
The markings on the upper leaf surface of this tiny plant are brown. The flowers are white.

General care: Top-dress with gravel or small pebbles to help keep the leaves dry.

Height: 3cm (1¼in) **Spread:** Indefinite

Temperature: Normal room

Humidity: Does best in dry air

Light: As much light and direct sun as possible

Watering: Very sparingly while in active growth from spring to autumn, and not at all during winter

Feeding: Not necessary

Propagation: Division of rootball

Pests and diseases: Trouble free, although plants will quickly rot if over-watered

Good companions: *Faucaria* species, *Ceropegia linearis* subsp. *woodii*

mammillaria

The majority of these easily grown cacti, which originate from the semi-desert areas between southern USA to northern South America, are spherical and densely covered with white, yellow or brown spines. In summer, white, yellow, pink or red, funnel-shaped flowers are produced in a ring around the top of the plant. Red berries often follow the blooms. These cacti tolerate temperatures down to 5°C (41°F), provided the compost is dry and the plants not too sappy. They are good for a sunny windowsill.

M. bombycina
This white wool-covered cactus bears pink flowers and produces offsets freely.

M. spinosissima
This species produces offsets which form a clump, eventually filling the pot. The flowers are pink.

Mammillaria spinosissima

M. zeilmanniana
In summer, even young plants of this clump-forming species bear flowers. These are deep pink with yellow stamens.

General care: Repot when the cactus body is 2cm (¾in) from the edge of the pot, using cactus compost. May be stood outdoors in summer.
Height: 15cm (6in) **Spread:** 25cm (10in)
Temperature: Cool room, minimum 5°C (41°F)
Humidity: Dry air
Light: Bright, including direct sun
Watering: Sparingly during active growth from spring to late summer, allowing the compost to dry out between watering. Keep almost dry in winter
Feeding: A couple of times in spring and summer, using a liquid feed at half strength
Propagation: Seed or division of rootball
Pests and diseases: Mealy bugs
Good companions: *Echinopsis* species, *Faucaria* species

maranta

Prayer plant
Native to Central and South American rainforests, these evergreen rhizomatous perennials require warmth, humidity and indirect light to thrive. The common name refers to the plant's habit of holding its leaves up vertically, rather like hands in prayer, at night.

M. leuconeura
The leaves of this initially upright and then spreading foliage plant are patterned with pale and dark green and silver lines. Those of herringbone plant (*M. leuconeura* var. *erythroneura*) have strongly defined pink veins and purple undersides. Rabbit's foot (*M. leuconeura* var. *kerchoveana*) has regular dark green markings on the leaves. All types produce spikes of small white flowers in spring and summer. Direct sun falling on the leaves will burn them.

General care: In warm weather mist plants with soft water. Repot every spring.
Height: 25cm (10in)
Spread: 30cm (12in)
Temperature: Normal room
Humidity: High
Light: Indirect
Watering: Moderately in spring and summer, sparingly at other times
Feeding: Monthly from spring to late summer
Propagation: Stem cuttings or division of rootball
Pests and diseases: Red spider mite
Good companions: *Calathea* species, *Ctenanthe* species

Maranta leuconeura var. *erythroneura*

monstera

The familiar Swiss cheese plant is the only member of this tropical genus from the Americas to be grown as a houseplant.

M. deliciosa Swiss cheese plant

The new leaves of this robust evergreen climber are entire and heart-shaped, only developing the characteristic holes and fingers as they mature. This tolerant, long-lived plant produces aerial roots along its stem. Once it exceeds about 75cm (2½ft) in height, it needs to be supported; a moss pole inserted in the pot works well.

General care: Sponge the leaves clean occasionally. Repot or top-dress every spring. Tuck in long aerial roots into the support or the compost.
Height: 3m (10ft) **Spread:** 1m (3ft)
Temperature: Minimum 15°C (60°F)
Humidity: Not too fussy, but benefits from regular misting

Light: Bright, with some direct sun. Tolerates poor light
Watering: Moderately in active growth, but sparingly in winter
Feeding: Monthly from spring to late summer
Propagation: Air layering or stem cuttings
Pests and diseases: Trouble free
Good companions: *Dracaena* species, *Ficus* species

Monstera deliciosa

musa

Banana
Most plants in this genus of evergreen, palm-like, suckering perennials are unsuitable for indoor cultivation, but given warm and humid conditions dwarf cultivars of *M. acuminata* can do well. Young banana plants make interesting and exotic specimens in the home but only produce fruit if grown in a warm conservatory.

M. acuminata 'Dwarf Cavendish'

This lush foliage plant is sometimes offered for sale in garden centres. It is a tropical tree-like plant with very large leaves that are often blotched purple.

General care: Clean the leaves occasionally, but avoid too much contact as they tear easily.
Height: 1.5m (5ft) **Spread:** 1m (3ft)
Temperature: Warm room, minimum 16°C (61°F)
Humidity: High
Light: Bright but indirect
Watering: Freely while in active growth, moderately at other times
Feeding: Monthly while in active growth
Propagation: Buy new plants
Pests and disease: Trouble free
Good companions: *Columnea* species, *Philodendron* species

Musa acuminata 'Dwarf Cavendish'

narcissus

Daffodil

The daffodil heralds the arrival of spring and is a lovely plant to have indoors, even though the display is short-lived. There are hundreds of varieties and most garden centres offer a good selection each autumn.

Buy varieties produced primarily for forcing indoors, such as *N. papyraceus* (syn. *N.* 'Paperwhite') or *N.* 'Soleil d'Or', and plant them close together with their 'noses' just showing above the compost. Keep them somewhere cool and move to their flowering position once the buds emerge in about eight weeks (see also page 46).

Alternatively, you can plant garden varieties and keep them in a cold, dark place (maybe a garage or shed) for 8–12 weeks or until the shoots emerge. Then move them to a cool bright position for flowering.

General care: Bulbs can be planted in the garden after flowering.
Height: 15–45cm (6–18in), depending on variety
Temperature: Normal room, but flowering is prolonged in a cool room

Narcissus papyraceus

Humidity: Not fussy
Light: Bright position once buds have formed
Watering: Keep compost just damp
Feeding: Not necessary
Propagation: Best to buy fresh bulbs
Pests and disease: Trouble free
Good companions: *Hyacinthus* cultivars

nertera

Only one species of this small genus of low creeping plants is cultivated. It is grown for its decorative fruits.

N. granadensis Bead plant

This mat-forming plant has tiny, cress-like leaves. In autumn it is covered with small orange berries, which follow the inconspicuous, greenish yellow flowers. Although it is a perennial plant, it is usually treated as an annual and discarded once the berries are past their best. If kept in a cool room, the display should last for a couple of months.

General care: No special requirement
Height: 5cm (2in) **Spread:** 15cm (6in)
Temperature: Cool room
Humidity: Mist occasionally
Light: Bright, including direct sun
Watering: Little and often as the roots are shallow
Feeding: Not necessary
Propagation: Division of rootball
Pests and diseases: Trouble free
Good companions: *Capsicum annuum* cultivars, *Oxalis tetraphylla*, *Senecio* species

Nertera granadensis

Nolina recurvata

nolina

This group of evergreen trees and shrubs from southern USA and Central America is frequently referred to as either *Beaucarnea* or *Nolina*, so you may need to look for it under both genus names at the garden centre.

N. recurvata (syn. Beaucarnea recurvata) Ponytail plant

The trunk of this Mexican tree swells out at the base and bears a tuft of curling linear leaves at the top. Young plants around 30cm (12in) tall are often available, but for real impact a 1.5m (5ft) specimen would make a handsome and impressive focal point that is both easy to care for and long-lived. The plant stores water in its swollen trunk so copes better with neglect than with over-watering.

General care: Repot or top-dress annually.

Height: 2m (6ft) **Spread** 1m (3ft)

Temperature: Normal room

Humidity: Not fussy

Light: Bright, including direct sun

Watering: Sparingly at all times

Feeding: Monthly while in active growth

Propagation: Division of offsets

Pests and disease: Trouble free

Good companions: *Cycas revoluta, Yucca elephantipes*

opuntia

Found throughout arid regions of the Americas, this is the largest cactus genus. Typically, opuntias have flattened pad-like stem sections held one above the other, although some species have cylindrical stems. Reluctant to flower indoors, they are grown for their interesting shapes. The spines arise from a dense tuft of tiny barbed bristles (glochids). These can be very decorative but are irritating if you get them in your skin; the best way of extracting them is to lightly dab your skin with sticky tape.

O. cylindrica

This columnar species has fat, needle-like leaves at the top of the stem.

O. microdasys

The rounded mid-green pads and yellow glochids, this species make an attractive addition to a cactus collection, as does

var. *albispina*, which has white glochids. Over time new pads grow from the tops of the older ones.

General care: Pad-forming species tend to grow outwards as well as upwards so plant them in terracotta pots for extra stability.

Height and spread: 30cm (12in)

Temperature: Normal room

Humidity: Thrives in dry air

Light: Bright, including direct sun

Watering: Sparingly in the growing season. In winter keep compost almost dry

Feeding: Once or twice in spring and summer, applying a liquid feed at half strength

Propagation: Remove a pad and allow the end to dry out and callus over for a couple of days before inserting it into gritty compost

Pests and diseases: Mealy bugs, scale insects

Good companions: *Echinopsis* species, *Faucaria* species

Opuntia species

oxalis

Only one of the more than 500 species of oxalis is grown as a houseplant. This large genus also includes some pernicious garden weeds.

O. tetraphylla (syn. O. deppei) Good luck plant, Lucky clover

The shamrock-like leaves of this bulbous mexican perennial are comprised of four triangular leaflets, which fold down at night. In summer, pink, funnel-shaped flowers, with a yellow throat, unfurl in the morning and close up in the evening.

Oxalis tetraphylla

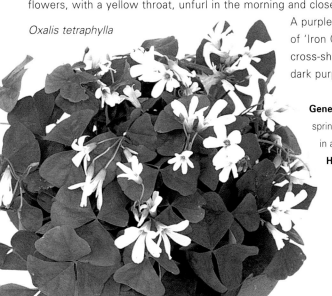

A purple mark on each leaflet of 'Iron Cross' forms a cross-shape. 'Purpurea' has dark purple foliage.

General care: Repot every spring. May be stood outdoors in a shady spot in summer.

Height and spread: 15cm (6in)

Temperature: Cold to normal room

Humidity: Not fussy

Light: Bright but indirect

Watering: Moderately

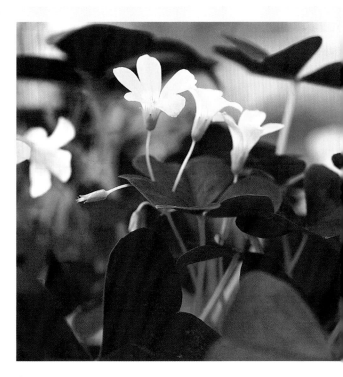

Oxalis tetraphylla 'Purpurea'

while in active growth, sparingly in winter

Feeding: Two or three times while in active growth

Propagation: Division of rootball

Pests and diseases: Trouble free

Good companions: *Asparagus* species, *Fatsia japonica*

orchids

With well over 20,000 species found in a wide range of habitats on every continent except Antarctica, orchids form one of the largest flowering plant families, exhibiting a huge diversity of form.

What makes orchids so distinctive is their unique flower structure. Typically, each flower is composed of three petal-like sepals and three petals, one of which, usually the lowest and known as the lip, is often shaped differently and distinctively marked.

The majority of orchids are found in tropical regions, where most grow as epiphytes (perching on trees), their dangling roots absorbing moisture and nutrients from the warm humid air. Orchids from temperate regions are often cultivated in the garden or a cool greenhouse, but tropical types are the best for use as houseplants. Most of the species described here will grow to 30–40cm (12–16in) in height and spread; some cymbidium cultivars, however, may reach 1m (3ft).

General care: Being such a diverse group of plants, the requirements for individuals will vary. There are, though, a few basic rules to follow. Keep out of direct light and cold draughts, and grow in a free-draining, bark-based orchid compost. This might be a mix of medium-coarse bark (not mulching bark) and perlite.

Temperature: See individual entries

Humidity: High. Stand on dampened pebbles

Light: Bright but indirect light, or as stated

Watering: Allow compost to dry out between thorough soakings, using rainwater or cooled boiled water. Water cymbidiums, oncidiums, dendrobiums and miltoniopsis sparingly during winter, when plant growth is reduced

Feeding: Apply an orchid fertiliser or a quarter-strength houseplant fertiliser at every third or fourth watering during the growing season

Progagation: Division of rootball, except for phalaenopsis, which can sometimes be propagated by offshoots or stem cuttings

Pests and diseases: Mealy bugs, scale insects

Cymbidium

These flower from autumn to spring and come in a wide range of colours. Cymbidiums orginate from India and China, and require a minimum temperature of 10°C (50°F). If conditions are too warm, they produce lots of dark green leaves but no flowers. Stand outdoors in dappled light during summer, to encourage initiation of flowers. Plants are dormant in late autumn and winter.

Dendrobium (phalaenopsis type)

This tropical orchid needs at least 16–18°C (61–65°F). It prefers good light and should not be allowed to dry out for long periods. The showy flowers are produced mostly in spring and last for up to six weeks.

Miltoniopsis
Pansy orchid

These multi-coloured orchids originate from central and southern America, where they grow in shaded, humid conditions. They do best in temperatures of 12–15°C (55–60°F), and their main flowering season is summer.

Cymbidium cultivar

Dendrobium cultivar

Miltoniopsis cultivar

Oncidium

Oncidiums are native to the forests of South America. As houseplants, they are best grown at 12–15°C (55–60°F) in moderate light. They usually experience a short period of dormancy. A number of hybrids are available, but yellow-flowered ones, which bloom mostly in summer, predominate. Oncidiums are sometimes referred to as 'dancing lady' flowers.

Paphiopedilum
Slipper orchid

Slipper orchids are so-called because of the distinctive pouch or slipper-shaped lip on the flower, which usually appears singly in winter and spring, from a rosette of plain or mottled leaves. Breeders have produced a range of colourful hybrids from these Asian orchids, which often grow on the forest floor in leaf litter. In cultivation they need a minimum of 13°C (56°F) in shaded, well-drained compost.

Phalaenopsis
Moth orchid

This orchid originates from tropical Asia and so requires a minimum temperature of 16–18°C (61–65°F). Phalaenopsis flower colours include white, pink, red and yellow, with varying degrees of spotting and stripes. White-flowered varieties are said to resemble a moth – hence this orchid's common name. Flowering can be at any time of the year and lasts for several weeks. If the top third of the flower stem is removed as the last few flowers fade, cutting the stem just above a joint or node, a new flower stem may be produced sooner than if the cut is made at the stem base. Phalaenopsis produces a few glossy, leathery leaves.

Phalaenopsis cultivar

Oncidium cultivar

Paphiopedilum cultivar

pachystachys

A single species in this genus of tropical evergreen shrubs and perennials is grown as a flowering houseplant. It is similar in appearance to the shrimp plant (*Justicia brandegeeana*), to which it is closely related.

P. lutea Lollipop plant

Throughout summer, this small shrub from Peru produces a cone-shaped flower head of overlapping golden-yellow bracts from which white tubular flowers emerge. The bracts remain decorative for several months.

General care: Plants become leggy and bare stemmed with age, so cut overwintered subjects back hard in early spring, and take cuttings every other year to create new plants.

Height and spread: 45cm (18in)

Temperature: Normal room

Humidity: High. Stand pots on trays of dampened pebbles

Light: Bright but indirect

Pachystachys lutea

Watering: Freely while in active growth, sparingly in winter

Feeding: Monthly from spring to late summer

Propagation: Stem cuttings

Pests and diseases: Red spider mite

Good companions: *Dieffenbachia* cultivars, *Justicia* species

pelargonium

Geranium

Pelargoniums fall into several groups, but as houseplants they are most easily divided into those grown for their flowers and for their scented foliage. Hundreds of cultivars of these evergreen perennials have been developed over the years.

Flowering geraniums

Zonal pelargoniums have succulent stems with leaves often marked with a purple-brown zone or variegation and bear large rounded clusters of blooms in an array of colours. They are available in flower in spring and early summer. Ivy-leaved pelargoniums have fleshy five-pointed leaves, brittle trailing stems and flowers in many shades. Available in flower in spring and early summer, they are useful for the front of containers. Regal pelargoniums have serrated leaves and large, often blotched or bi-coloured flowers. They are grown primarily as indoor flowering pot plants, even in winter.

Scented-leaved geraniums

These plants are grown for the scent their foliage releases, especially when handled. In warm weather they exude their fragrance without even being touched.

General care: Snap off faded flowers where the stalk meets the stem. Cut back the plant by half in spring – the cut material can be used as cuttings to start new plants. Foliage types in particular get leggy, and their shoot tips should be pinched out frequently to keep them bushy.

Height and spread: 30–60cm (1–2ft)

Temperature: Normal room

Humidity: Not fussy

Light: Bright, including direct sun

Watering: Keep moist while in active growth from spring to summer; in winter just enough to stop compost drying out

Feeding: Monthly from spring to late summer

Propagation: Stem cuttings

Pests and diseases: Grey mould, aphids

Good companions: *Abutilon* species, *Cissus discolor*

Ivy-leaved pelargonium

Over a thousand peperomia species occur throughout tropical and sub-tropical regions. Many of these small evergreen perennials make excellent houseplants and are grown for their fleshy leaves, which may be puckered, shiny or hairy, and marbled or blotched. Spikes of tiny white flowers are produced in late summer. Peperomias thrive in warm, humid conditions, but dislike being very wet at the roots.

P. argyreia
The spoon-shaped leaves are marked with silver between the veins.

P. caperata
The dark green, heart-shaped leaves are deeply wrinkled. Tiny white flowers are borne on 5–8cm (2–3in) spikes. 'Luna Red' has purple leaves held on red stalks. 'Lilian' has unusual crested flower spikes.

P. obtusifolia 'Greengold'
This plant has large, shiny, bright green leaves, broadly edged with yellowish green.

peperomia

General care: Avoid wetting the leaves when watering.
Height and spread: 20cm (8in)
Temperature: Normal room, minimum 10°C (50°F)
Humidity: Moderate to high
Light: Indirect light. Green-leaved varieties are fairly tolerant of low light levels
Watering: Moderately while in active growth, sparingly at other times
Feeding: Monthly while in active growth
Propagation: Stalked leaf cuttings
Pests and diseases: Trouble free
Good companions: *Calathea* species, *Schefflera* species

Peperomia caperata 'Lilian'

philodendron

Belonging to a large genus of evergreen rainforest shrubs and climbers, many philodendrons are grown indoors for the tropical quality of their foliage. One of the most beautiful is *P. selloum*, which has huge, deeply incised leaves but is too big for the average home. Some of the climbing species are useful where space is tight, as they cling closely to their moss-pole supports.

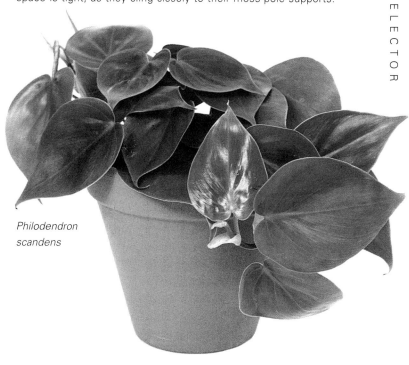

Philodendron scandens

P. erubescens 'Burgundy'
Large, coppery purple leaves on dark red stalks distinguish this slow-growing climber.

P. melanochrysum
Black gold philodendron, Velour philodendron
This sparsely branched climber from Colombia has heart-shaped, slightly felted, dark green leaves with pale veins. Grown up a moss pole, it will attach itself with aerial roots.

P. scandens Sweetheart plant
Similar to *P. melanochrysum*, this climber from Mexico has glossy dark green leaves, which may be red-purple beneath.

General care: Clean leaves regularly. Repot or top-dress with fresh compost every spring.
Height: 1.5m (5ft) **Spread:** 4m (12ft)
Temperature: Warm room, minimum 15°C (60°F)
Humidity: Moderate to high
Light: Tolerates low light levels
Watering: Keep compost moist while in active growth. Water sparingly in winter
Feeding: Monthly while in active growth
Propagation: Stem cuttings or simple layering
Pests and diseases: Mealy bugs, red spider mite, scale insects
Good companions: *Cissus* species, *Monstera deliciosa*

palms

Tolerant of dry air, poor light levels and erratic watering, many palms make excellent houseplants, and they are unrivalled in their ability to introduce a tropical feel into a room.

Palms come mostly from tropical and sub-tropical regions of the world. A few species, such as *Chamaerops humilis*, are native to warm temperate regions, such as the Mediterranean, and can be grown outdoors in areas with mild winters.

All palms have a single growing point at the top of the stem and will begin to die if this is damaged, which is why they cannot be pruned, other than to remove yellowing leaves. However, as they are so slow-growing they are unlikely to outgrow their allotted space, and even well-grown specimens will not produce more than two or three new leaves each year. A specimen growing in optimum conditions is likely to reach 1.5m (5ft) tall.

All the palms described here are native to tropical forest floors, where the light they receive is filtered through the tree canopy above. For this reason they are useful for rooms that do not receive a great deal of sun.

General care: Exposure to summer showers is the best way to clean dust and dirt from the leaves, so if possible stand palms outside in a sheltered, shady spot for a month or so.

Temperature: Normal room, minimum 12°C (54°F), except phoenix, which prefers minimum 15°C (60°F)

Humidity: Although their native environments are humid, palms tolerate dry air well, but should not be positioned near radiators as this will make the leaf tips go brown

Light: Bright but indirect

Watering: Moderately while in active growth from spring to late summer, ideally allowing compost to become quite dry between watering. In winter, apply just enough water to prevent compost drying out completely

Feeding: Monthly from spring to late summer, applying a moderate amount of weak liquid feed

Propagation: Division of rootball for suckering genera such as rhapis, caryota and chamaedorea. Seed for others, although this may be hard to find

Pests and diseases: Red spider mite, especially where humidity is low. Mealy bugs and scale insects may also be troublesome

Caryota mitis

Chamaedorea elegans

Cocos nucifera

Howea fosteriana

Caryota mitis
Fish-tail palm

Caryotas are native to South-East Asia, where they are a source of palm wine and sago. *C. mitis* is a suckering species with arching fronds and leaflets that resemble fish tails. *C. urens* is similar but single stemmed.

Chamaedorea elegans
Parlour palm

Widely available and easily grown, the parlour palm is often offered for sale as a clump of potted seedlings. Unusually for a palm it is quite free flowering, with mature specimens producing sprays of small yellow flowers. As a houseplant it seldom grows more than 1m (3ft) tall.

Cocos nucifera
Coconut palm

This interesting specimen plant is unfortunately invariably short-lived, as it requires tropical greenhouse conditions to survive in the long term. The nut is planted to half its depth in compost and the elegant fronds emerge from an 'eye' at one end.

Howea fosteriana
Kentia palm, Thatch leaf palm

Popular as a houseplant since Victorian times, this graceful plant and the very similar *H. belmoreana* are native to Lord Howe Island, off the east coast of Australia. Both are tolerant of neglect.

Phoenix canariensis
Canary Island date palm

Young specimens are good plants where space is limited, as the stiff leaves are initially held upright before arching out on older plants. The slender-trunked *P. roebelenii* makes a graceful focal point and is a good air purifier.

Rhapis excelsa

This tolerant and easy-care palm forms a clump of upright stems and produces fan-shaped leaves divided into blunt leaflets. It grows in low light levels and is good for removing the common household toxin formaldehyde from the air (see page 115).

Washingtonia filifera
Desert fan, Petticoat palm

Native to California and Arizona, where it is used as a street tree, the fan-shaped leaves of this palm are edged with curling, thread-like filaments.

Washingtonia filifera

Phoenix canariensis

Rhapis excelsa

pilea

Members of this tropical rainforest genus thrive in warm humid conditions. Those grown as houseplants have strikingly textured and patterned leaves. Young plants produce the best foliage, so take cuttings every other year to create new plants.

P. cadierei Aluminium plant
The dark green leaves of this upright evergreen perennial are neatly patterned with silver. 'Minima' is just 15cm (6in) tall.

P. involucrata 'Moon Valley'
This compact cultivar has puckered, bronze-green leaves with purple sunken veins.

P. microphylla Artillery plant
The tiny, slightly succulent bright, green leaves of this fern-like pilea are carried on fleshy stems.

General care: Clean leaves regularly, standing plants with rough-textured leaves outdoors during a summer shower. Pinch out shoots to encourage bushiness.
Height: 30cm (12in)
Spread 20cm (8in)
Temperature: Normal room

Humidity: Moderate to high
Light: Tolerates low light levels
Watering: Moderately while in active growth, sparingly at other times
Feeding: Monthly from spring to late summer
Propagation: Stem cuttings
Pests and diseases: Trouble free
Good companions: *Fittonia* species, *Hypoestes phyllostachya*

Pilea cultivar

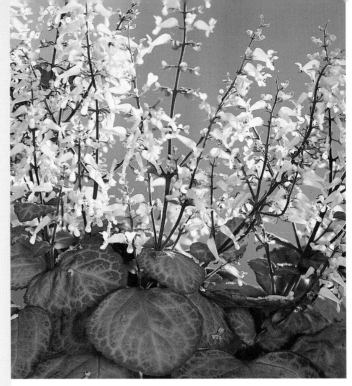

Plectranthus oertendahlii 'Silver Star'

plectranthus

These shrubby or trailing plants from Africa, Asia and Australia are sometimes grown as summer bedding in hanging baskets. Those mentioned here have aromatic variegated foliage. Place them on a shelf in terracotta rather than plastic containers, otherwise their trailing foliage may cause them to topple over.

P. forsteri 'Marginatus' (syn. P. coleoides 'Marginatus')
The leaves of this upright then trailing evergreen perennial are aromatic when crushed and have white, scalloped leaf edges. Plants intermittently produce spikes of tubular white flowers.

P. madagascariensis 'Variegated Mintleaf'
Similar to *P. forsteri* 'Marginatus', the slightly fleshy leaves smell of mint when they are crushed.

P. oertendahlii
This trailing perennial has reddish stems. The scallop-edged leaves are bright green with silver-white veins above and purple felted undersides. 'Silver Star' is a free-flowering cultivar producing spikes of white flowers in spring and summer.

General care: Pinch out shoot tips to encourage bushiness.
Height: 25cm (10in) **Spread** 60cm (2ft)
Temperature: Normal room
Humidity: Not fussy
Light: Bright, including direct sun
Watering: Freely when in active growth, sparingly in winter
Feeding: Monthly from spring to late summer
Propagation: Stem cuttings, which root easily in a glass of water
Pests and diseases: Trouble free
Good companions: *Abutilon* species, *Heliotropium arborescens* cultivars

primula

Primrose

The majority of this large genus of mainly herbaceous perennials come from a range of habitats in the Northern Hemisphere. The plants mentioned here are available in winter and spring and are best regarded as temporary houseplants for bringing a splash of colour into the home.

P. obconica

Loose clusters of large, slightly fragrant flowers are held above the foliage. The white, pink, lilac or red blooms often have a contrasting green eye. Contact with the foliage may cause skin problems in some people, although 'Touch Me' should not.

P. vulgaris cultivars

Numerous cultivars of this compact primrose have brightly coloured blooms from white through yellow and red to blue, usually have a contrasting yellow eye. The flowers are held low in the centre of the rosette of foliage, but in the Polyanthus Group, which is also derived from *P. vulgaris*, they are generally carried cowslip-like on stalks above the foliage.

General care: Deadhead to prolong flowering. Keeping plants in a cool room will also prolong flowering. *P. vulgaris* cultivars can be planted in the garden after flowering.

Height and spread: 20cm (8in)

Temperature: Cool to normal room

Humidity: Not fussy

Light: Bright, including direct sun

Watering: Keep compost moist

Feeding: Not necessary

Propagation: Seed, or buy new plants

Pests and diseases: Trouble free

Good companions: *Campanula isophylla, Cyclamen persicum* cultivars

Primula obconica

Radermachera sinica

radermachera

Native to Taiwan, *R. sinica* is the only species in this genus to be cultivated as a houseplant. The main bonus of this plant is its tolerance of dry air in centrally heated rooms. The foliage remains lustrous where other plant leaf tips would go brown. It is a vigorous shrub and will put on a good amount of growth if repotted annually. In the wild this plant bears scented yellow flowers but it is unlikely to produce these on pot-grown specimens.

R. sinica

This easy-going little evergreen shrub is grown for its glossy leaves and graceful branching habit. It is currently enjoying a resurgence in popularity and is often sold in supermarkets.

General care: Pinch out the shoots to promote bushy growth. Repot each spring.

Height: 1m (3ft) **Spread:** 80cm (2ft 6in)

Temperature: Normal to warm room

Humidity: Not fussy

Light: Bright but indirect

Watering: Keep compost moist at all times

Feeding: Monthly while in active growth between spring and autumn

Propagation: Stem cuttings

Pests and diseases: Trouble free

Good companions: *Dracaena* species, *Ficus* species

rhododendron

Numerous garden shrubs prized for their beautiful flowers are members of this very large genus. Most are unsuited to indoor cultivation, but *R. simsii* hybrids are sold specifically as flowering evergreen houseplants for winter and early spring. Kept cool and moist, they provide a glorious display for up to two months.

R. simsii hybrids Azalea

Naturally spring flowering, these azaleas are often forced for Christmas use. Modern hybrids produce a mass of ruffled or double, white, pink, red or bi-coloured flowers that almost obscure the foliage. Although they cannot tolerate frost, they will rapidly die if kept too warm, so a porch, hall or stairwell is generally the best site for them.

General care: To keep plants for a second year, repot in mid-spring using ericaceous (lime-free) compost and sink the pot in a shady garden bed. Return it to a cool room before the first frosts.

Height and spread: 30cm (12in)

Temperature: Cold or cool room, ideally 7–15°C (45–60°F)

Humidity: Not fussy as long as the temperature is low

Light: Bright but indirect

Watering: Keep compost constantly moist. Rainwater or cooled boiled tap water is best

Rhododendron simsii hybrid

Feeding: Occasionally while in flower. Plants that are being kept for a second year should also be fed throughout summer

Propagation: Stem cuttings

Pests and diseases: Trouble free

Good companions: *Aucuba japonica*, *Euonymus japonicus* cultivars

saintpaulia

African violet

Native to tropical East Africa, this is a small genus of low-growing, rosette-forming perennials. Countless cultivars of *S. ionantha* are available (the species itself is rarely grown) with a variety of flower shapes and colours. Plants are usually sold without a cultivar name, so if you want one in particular you will need to go to a specialist nursery. African violets can be kept from year to year but are commonly treated as temporary pot plants and discarded after flowering.

S. ionantha cultivars

These plants are available in flower almost all year round and produce blooms over a long period, especially in spring and summer. Flowers may be white, mauve, pink, purple or blue with a yellow eye, and many have ruffled or double petals. The rosettes are hairy leaved.

General care: Repot every other year into a slightly larger pot – too large a pot will produce foliar growth at the expense of flowers. Cut off spent flowers and damaged leaves.

Height: 10cm (4in) **Spread:** 20cm (8in)

Temperature: Warm room, minimum 18°C (64°F)

Humidity: High. Stand plants on dampened pebbles

Light: Bright but indirect

Saintpaulia ionantha cultivar

Watering: Moderately, allowing the compost to dry out slightly between watering. Pour water into the dish under the plant to avoid wetting the leaves

Feeding: From spring to late summer using a liquid feed at half strength

Propagation: Stalked leaf cuttings

Pests and diseases: Crown rot, grey mould, mealy bugs or division of rootball

Good companions: *Sinningia* cultivars, *Streptocarpus* cultivars

sansevieria

Native to dry rocky regions of tropical Africa and India, this genus contains some tough low-maintenance houseplants. They are cultivated for their stiff, sword-like or cylindrical leaves, which grow upright from a rhizome and may be banded or variegated. The simple silhouettes look good in modern interiors and taller types are useful for adding vertical accents to plant groupings.

S. cylindrica
The dark green cylindrical stems of this striking plant are held in a V shape.

S. trifasciata 'Laurentii' Mother-in-law's tongue
The erect, sword-shaped leaves have irregular cross bands and yellow edges. 'Hahnii' is a dwarf cultivar, with a flat rosette of broadly yellow-margined leaves, and a height and spread of 15cm (6in).

General care: Repot only when pot-bound. Terracotta or stone pots provide extra stability for tall varieties. Be careful not to damage the leaf tips as this can stop the leaf growing.

Height: 75cm (2½ft)

Spread: 30cm (12in)

Temperature: Normal room

Humidity: Tolerates dry air

Light: Bright, including direct sun, for best growth, but tolerates lower light levels

Watering: Moderately while in active growth in spring and summer, sparingly at other times

Feeding: Monthly from spring to late summer, applying a liquid feed at half strength

Propagation: Division of offsets or midrib leaf cuttings

Pests and diseases: Trouble free

Good companions: *Crassula* species, *Haworthia* species

Sansevieria trifasciata 'Laurentii'

Saxifrages are primarily cushion-forming alpine perennials and many make pretty additions to a rock garden, but only one species can be grown indoors.

S. stolonifera
Mother of thousands
This rosette or tuft-forming plant bears rounded hairy leaves with white veins and red undersides. The common name refers to the abundant plantlets that form on the end of long trailing running stems known as stolons. It is best grown in a hanging basket so that these can dangle attractively. In summer, loose clusters of small white flowers are produced on long stems. 'Tricolor' has pink-and-cream leaf edges.

saxifraga

General care: No particular requirements.

Trailing height and spread: 20cm (8in), but the stolons may be 75cm (2½ft) long

Temperature: Cold to normal room

Humidity: Mist occasionally, especially in warm weather

Light: Bright but indirect

Watering: Freely while in active growth, sparingly in winter

Feed: Monthly from spring to late summer

Propagation: Division of plantlets

Pests and diseases: Aphids

Good companions: *Araucaria heterophylla*, *Campanula* cultivars

Saxifraga stolonifera

schefflera

Several foliage houseplants belong to this large genus of air-purifying, evergreen tropical shrubs, trees and climbers. All are large trees in the wild, but the species mentioned here are unlikely to exceed 1.5m (5ft) indoors. They can be kept smaller by cutting off the top. All resent draughts and temperature fluctuations, but tolerate erratic watering.

S. arboricola
Each glossy leaf of this upright species comprises 7–15 oval leaflets. 'Aurea' has heavily yellow-variegated leaves but needs good light to maintain this colouring.

S. elegantissima (syn. Dizygotheca elegantissima)
The long, slender, coppery green leaflets of this elegant houseplant are toothed and held horizontally.

Schefflera arboricola 'Aurea'

General care: Turn the plants regularly to stop them leaning towards the light. Clean leaves regularly. Repot every spring.
Height: 1m (3ft) **Spread:** 50cm (20in)
Temperature: Normal room
Humidity: Mist leaves in warm weather, especially *S. elegantissima*, which requires higher humidity to stop the leaves going brown at the tips

Light: Bright but indirect
Watering: Freely when in active growth, moderately in winter
Feeding: Monthly when in active growth
Propagation: Stem cuttings
Pests and diseases: Red spider mite, scale insects
Good companions: *Codiaeum* cultivars, *Ficus* species

schlumbergera

Christmas cactus
Native to the rainforests of Brazil, this small spineless genus seems an unlikely member of the cactus family, but its arching stems are made up of numerous flattened fleshy segments. In winter, large brilliantly coloured flowers are produced singly or in pairs from the end segments. Many schlumbergeras are epiphytic (they perch on trees) and so look good in a hanging basket, displaying the exotic-looking flowers near eye level. In the wild these forest cacti are pollinated by hummingbirds.

S. truncata (syn. Zygocactus truncatus)
This species bears cerise flowers from late autumn to winter. Along with *S. x buckleyi*, it provides the origins of many variously coloured modern hybrids, such as white-flowered 'Wintermärchen' and 'Gold Charm' with its pinky yellow blooms.

General care: Repot or top-dress every spring. Do not move plants once buds have formed as they may be aborted.
Height and spread: 30cm (12in)
Temperature: Normal room
Humidity: Mist plants regularly
Light: Bright but indirect
Watering: Moderately while in active growth, sparingly in winter

Feeding: Monthly from spring to late summer, using a liquid feed at half strength
Propagation: Stem cuttings
Pests and diseases: Mealy bugs
Good companions: *Sedum morganianum*, *Senecio rowleyanus*

Schlumbergera truncata cultivar

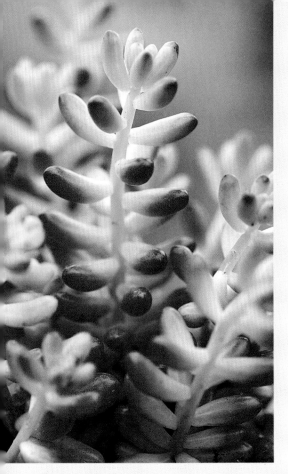

sedum

Species of sedum that are grown as houseplants are typically small and succulent, admired for their plump, often colourful leaves. They associate particularly well with other succulents and are easy plants for a sunny windowsill. They resent being wet at the roots, especially in winter, and will rot if the soil is waterlogged.

S. morganianum   Donkey's tail
Fragile trailing stems up to 45cm (18in) long are packed with grey-green leaves.

S. pachyphyllum
The blue-green, cylindrical leaves of this upright species are tipped with red.

S. x rubrotinctum
The sausage-shaped leaves of this upright then trailing plant flush red in sun.

General care: When repotting or top-dressing in spring use a soil-based compost with added grit to improve drainage.
Height: 20cm (8in) **Spread:** 25cm (10in)
Temperature: Cool to normal room
Humidity: Tolerates dry air
Light: Bright, including direct sun

Watering: Moderately from spring to late summer, very sparingly at other times
Feeding: Two or three times in the growing season
Propagation: Slashed leaf cuttings or stem cuttings
Pests and diseases: Mealy bugs
Good companions: *Crassula* species

Sedum x rubrotinctum

senecio

Two very different species of this large and diverse genus are grown as houseplants. One, cape ivy, is a climber and the other, string of beads, a trailing succulent. Another houseplant that used to be part of this genus was *S. cruentus*, commonly known as cineraria (see page 17). This flowering pot plant has been reclassified as *Pericallis x hybrida*, but plants are generally sold under the common name.

S. macroglossus 'Variegatus'   Cape ivy
This ivy-leaved evergreen twining shrub is good for a hanging basket as well as scrambling up a support. In favourable climates, it may bear pale yellow blooms.

General care: Trim back over-long shoots as necessary. Repot every spring.
Height: 80cm (2.6ft) **Spread:** 50cm (20in)
Temperature: Normal room
Humidity: Tolerates dry air
Light: Bright, including direct sun
Watering: Moderately while in active growth, sparing at other times
Feeding: Monthly from spring to late summer
Propagation: Cuttings
Pests and diseases: Trouble free
Good companions: *Abutilon* cultivars, *Cissus discolor*

Senecio rowleyanus

S. rowleyanus   String of beads
The succulent spherical leaves of this trailing plant resemble peas and makes a good specimen for a hanging basket.

General care: Too fragile to be repotted, mature specimens need occasional feeding.
Trailing height: 60cm (2ft) **Spread:** 25cm (10in)
Temperature: Normal room
Humidity: Tolerates dry air
Light: Bright but indirect
Watering: Moderately while in active growth, sparingly in winter
Feeding: Two or three times while in active growth using a liquid feed at half strength
Propagation: Stem cuttings
Pests and diseases: Mealy bugs
Good companions: *Ceropegia linearis* subsp. *woodii*, *Sedum morganianum*

sinningia

The genus includes about 40 shrubs and tuberous perennials from Central and South American tropical forests, but only *S. speciosa* hybrids are widely grown as flowering houseplants.

S. speciosa hybrids Gloxinia

These tuberous perennials form rosettes of large felted leaves and over a long period in summer bear exotic bell-shaped flowers, which may be white, pink, red or purple and sometimes bi-coloured or speckled. Specialist nurseries offer a range: 'Hollywood' has purple flowers, 'Waterloo' bears velvety dark red blooms, and 'Mont Blanc' has white flowers. Gloxinias die down after flowering but can be made to flower the following year.

General care: When plants begin to die back in autumn, remove the yellowing top growth and store the tubers in their pots until the following spring. Then repot and resume watering.
Height and spread: 25cm (10in)
Temperature: Normal to warm room
Humidity: High
Light: Bright but indirect
Watering: Freely while in active growth, reducing the amount in autumn as the leaves yellow and begin to die back
Feeding: Monthly while in active growth
Propagation: Stalked leaf cuttings
Pests and diseases: Trouble free
Good companions: *Saintpaulia* cultivars, *Streptocarpus* cultivars

Sinningia speciosa hybrid

solanum

The best-known plant in this diverse genus of 1400 species is the potato (*S. tuberosum*). Two solanum species are cultivated as houseplants for their attractive fruits, which provide a cheerful winter display for many weeks. Both are available in autumn and winter, as their spherical berries start to ripen to red. The inedible fruits last best in a cool room, and once they shrivel the plant can be discarded. All parts of both plants cause severe discomfort if ingested.

S. capsicastrum Winter cherry

This evergreen shrub has closely arranged, slightly hairy leaves and downy stems. The white flowers have orange-yellow stamens and are followed by green berries, which mature to an orange-red colour.

S. pseudocapsicum
Christmas cherry, Winter cherry

Similar to *S. capsicastrum* this has slightly larger, redder and longer-lasting berries, and it is easier to grow. Dwarf varieties are also available.

General care: Keep plants out of the reach of small children.
Height and spread: 35cm (14in)
Temperature: Cold to cool room
Humidity: Not fussy in a cool room, but mist regularly in a warm room
Light: Bright, including direct sun
Watering: Keep compost moist at all times
Feeding: Not necessary
Propagation: Stem cuttings
Pests and diseases: Trouble free
Good companions: *Capsicum annuum*, *Chrysanthemum* cultivars

Solanum pseudocapsicum

soleirolia

Mind-your-own-business
This single species genus
is useful for rooms with low
light levels, and can also be
used for underplanting in
larger pots, where it will quickly
spread to form a living mulch.
Native to Corsica, soleirolia can
be an invasive garden weed in
mild climates.

S. soleirolii (syn. Helxine soleirolii)
The tiny leaves of this low,
creeping, stem-rooting perennial
are green, while those of the cultivars
'Aurea' and 'Variegata' are yellow-green
and silver variegated respectively.

General care: As these plants are
usually sold spilling over the edge
of the pot, it is a good idea to
repot them on as soon as you
get them home.
Height: 5cm (2in)
Spread: Indefinite
Temperature: Cool room
Humidity: Moderate to high
Light: Tolerates low light levels
Watering: Keep compost moist at all times
Feeding: Twice during spring and summer
Propagation: Division of rootball
Pests and diseases: Trouble free
Good companions: x *Fatshedera lizei*,
Tolmiea menziesii

Soleirolia soleirolii

solenostemon

Coleus, Flame nettle, Painted nettle
Specimens of this genus of about 60 evergreen, sub-shrubby perennials
from tropical Africa and Asia are cultivated for their colourful foliage.
They are easy plants for a sunny windowsill and useful for enlivening
plain green foliage displays. The most commonly available are hybrids
derived from *S. scutellarioides*.

S. scutellarioides hybrids
Succulent square stems support a wide variety of leaf shapes and
colours, including yellow, pink, purple and brown, often with several
colours on one leaf. Plants tend to deteriorate over time but are very
easily raised from cuttings. Hard pruning in spring also stimulates
fresh new growth.

General care: Pinch out shoot tips and the small flower spikes that appear at
the top of the shoots to encourage bushy growth.
Height: 50cm (20in) **Spread:** 30cm (12in)
Temperature: Normal room
Humidity: Moderate to high
Light: Bright, including direct sun on all but the hottest summer days
Watering: Freely while in active growth, sparingly in winter
Feeding: Monthly from spring to late summer
Propagation: Stem cuttings or seed
Pests and diseases: Mealy bugs
Good companions: *Catharanthus roseus*, *Iresine* cultivars

Solenostemon scutellarioides hybrid

spathiphyllum

Peace lily

Exotic, white, flower-like structures, made up of a curved oval spathe and knobbly spadix, are the attraction of these easily grown houseplants. The main flowering season is spring and summer, but the long-lived blooms may be produced intermittently throughout the year. These rhizomatous evergreen perennials are native to the damp tropical forests of Indonesia and South America, so those grown as houseplants need to be kept well watered. They are useful for dark rooms and also effective for removing the common household toxin formaldehyde from the air (see page 115).

S. 'Mauna Loa'

This hybrid has large flower-like structures and lustrous foliage.

S. wallisii

Similar to *S.* 'Mauna Loa', this species is shorter, growing to only 30cm (12in).

Spathiphyllum wallisii

General care: Clean leaves regularly. Snip out old flowers and yellowing leaves. Repot every spring.
Height: 60cm (2ft) **Spread:** 30cm (12in)
Temperature: Normal room
Humidity: Moderate to high
Light: Bright but indirect, also tolerates poor light

Watering: Keep compost moist at all times
Feeding: Monthly from spring to late summer
Propagation: Division of rootstock
Pests and diseases: Trouble free
Good companions: *Anthurium* cultivars, *Monstera deliciosa*

Streptocarpus hybrid

streptocarpus

Cape primrose

The free-flowering annuals and perennials of this genus originate mostly in South Africa. Most grown as houseplants are hybrids and generally have larger and more showy flowers than the species. All resent being permanently wet at the roots and will quickly rot if over-watered.

S. hybrids

Funnel-shaped flowers in a range of colours from white through pink and red to blue are borne in clusters above the low rosette of primrose-like leaves. They are mainly produced from spring to autumn, although there are some modern hybrids in flower at all times of the year. Good varieties include 'Emily', with yellow-throated lilac-pink flowers, 'Heidi' with purple-marked blue flowers, and the white-flowered 'Albatross'.

General care: Cut off spent flowers. Repot every other year in spring, using a soil-less compost.
Height: 30cm (12in) **Spread** 35cm (14in)
Temperature: Normal room
Humidity: High
Light: Bright but indirect. Avoid south-facing windowsills

Watering: Moderate at all times, allowing the compost to dry out between watering
Feeding: Fortnightly
Propagation: Midrib leaf cuttings or division of rootball
Pests and diseases: Mealy bugs
Good companions: *Saintpaulia* cultivars

stromanthe

The rhizomatous herbaceous perennials of this small tropical Central and South American genus are closely related to (and often confused with) ctenanthe and calathea. One species of stromanthe is grown as a foliage houseplant, its vibrantly coloured leaves making a dramatic focal point.

S. sanguinea

This densely clump-forming, upright plant produces the large glossy leaves marked green and white above and brilliant pink below. It needs high humidity to prevent its leaf tips from turning brown. Vigorous 'Triostar' is the cultivar most often seen.

General care: Clean leaves regularly. Plants are often sold in pots that are too small for them, so benefit from being potted on immediately you get them home.
Height: 60cm (2ft)
Spread: 40cm (16in)
Temperature: Normal room
Humidity: Moderate to high
Light: Bright but indirect

Watering: Freely while in active growth, sparingly at other times. The leaf edges begin to curl inwards when the plant is too dry
Feeding: Monthly while in active growth
Propagation: Division of rootball
Pests and diseases: Trouble free
Good companions: *Anthurium* cultivars, *Ctenanthe* cultivars

These evergreen perennial climbers from tropical regions of Central and South America are cultivated for their attractive leaves, which start off heart-shaped but develop three or five lobes as they mature. While the plants themselves are tolerant of low light levels, any leaf variegation will become poor.

syngonium

S. podophyllum Goosefoot

Usually offered for sale as a short young plant, this climber can be grown up a moss pole or allowed to trail. Juvenile leaves have the best colouring, so you may wish to keep the plant bushy by snipping out the climbing stems. Various cultivars are available, including 'White Butterfly', with leaves that are nearly all white, 'Emerald Gem', with white leaf veins, and 'Variegatum', with cream splashes.

General care: Clean leaves regularly. Plants produce aerial roots but if grown up a moss pole the stems need to be tied in.
Height: 1.5m (5ft)
Spread: 50cm (20in)
Temperature: Normal room
Humidity: Moderate to high
Light: Bright but indirect
Watering: Freely while in active growth, moderately at other times
Feeding: Monthly while in active growth
Propagation: Stem cuttings
Pests and diseases: Red spider mite
Good companions: *Monstera deliciosa*, *Philodendron* species

Stromanthe sanguinea 'Triostar'

Syngonium podophyllum 'Emerald Gem'

tolmiea

Pick-a-back plant, Piggyback plant
The common names for this single species genus refer to the plant's habit of producing plantlets on the top of mature leaves. Native to western North America, it is tolerant of low temperatures, so is a useful plant for porches. It can also be grown outdoors once it has been hardened off.

T. menziesii

In late spring this hairy-leaved, clump-forming perennial may produce small whitish flowers. The leaves are pale to lime-green, but those of 'Taff's Gold', the most popular variety, have yellow patches and speckles.

General care: Repot annually until plants begin to look shabby, then raise new stock.
Height: 30cm (12in) **Spread** 45cm (18in)
Temperature: Cool to normal room
Humidity: Not fussy
Light: Bright but indirect
Watering: Freely while in active growth, more moderately at other times

Feeding: Monthly from spring to late summer
Propagation: Division of plantlets
Pests and diseases: Trouble free
Good companions: *Fatsia* cultivars, *Soleirolia* cultivars

Tolmiea menziesii 'Taff's Gold'

tradescantia

Three virtually indestructible plants in this genus of evergreen perennials are grown for their variegated leaves and trailing habit, which suits a hanging basket particularly well.

T. cerinthoides 'Variegata'
The slightly fleshy, hairy leaves are striped cream.

T. fluminensis 'Albovittata' Inch plant, Wandering jew
The upper leaves are boldly marked with white and, like the green-leaved species, flushed purple on the underside. 'Aurea' has yellow stripes, and 'Quicksilver', which is particularly vigorous, is evenly striped with green and white.

T. zebrina
Similar to *T. fluminensis*, the upper leaf surface has a pair of silver stripes and a metallic sheen, while the underside is purple-pink. Vigorous 'Purpusii' has purple-flushed leaves.

General care: Remove any shoots with plain green leaves. When plants become straggly, take cuttings and discard the parent.
Height: 60cm (2ft) **Spread:** 30cm (12in)
Temperature: Normal room
Humidity: Not fussy
Light: Bright, including direct sun

Watering: Freely while in active growth, sparingly in winter
Feeding: Monthly from spring to late summer
Propagation: Stem cuttings
Pests and diseases: Trouble free
Good companions: *Codiaeum* cultivars, *Dracaena* cultivars

Tradescantia fluminensis 'Albovittata'

yucca

Yuccas are evergreen shrubs and trees from hot and dry areas of North and Central America. One species in particular is prized as a foliage houseplant for its crown of spiky leaves. Tolerant of both dry air and irregular watering, it is easy to grow and can be very long-lived.

Y. elephantipes

The lance-shaped leaves arise from around the top of the trunk, which is technically a big cutting. Large specimens make dramatic and exotic focal points, but these very slow-growing plants take a long time to attain their mature height.

General care: Wipe the leaves down occasionally. Repot when the plant becomes top-heavy.
Height: 1.5m (5ft) **Spread:** 60cm (2ft)
Temperature: Normal room
Humidity: Not fussy
Light: Bright, including direct sun
Watering: Moderately during active growth in spring and summer, sparingly at other times. It will not suffer if it dries out completely
Feeding: Two or three times in the growing season
Propagation: If the crown is congested, you can cut off a side shoot and use it as a stem cutting, otherwise buy new plants
Pests and diseases: Trouble free
Good companions: *Cordyline* species, *Ficus* species

Yucca elephantipes

zamioculcas

This tropical and sub-tropical genus from east and south-east Africa contains just one species, which is now widely available as a foliage plant. It is easy to grow and has a fascinating architectural quality that lends itself to modern and minimalist interiors.

Z. zamiifolia

With upright succulent stems and thick glossy leaves held in two neat rows, this plant is sturdy and undemanding as long as it receives a lot of light.

General care:
Wipe the leaves regularly to keep them shiny.
Height: 1.2m (4ft)
Spread: 60cm (2ft)
Temperature: Normal room
Humidity: Not fussy
Light: Bright, including direct sun
Watering: Sparingly at all times. Allow the compost to become quite dry between watering
Feeding: Monthly from spring to late summer with a liquid feed at half strength
Propagation:
Division of rootball
Pests and diseases: Trouble free
Good companions: *Cycas revoluta*, *Nolina recurvata*

Zamioculcas zamiifolia

choosing the best plants

The following plant lists draw on all the houseplants described in the preceding pages of the Plant Selector, but they are grouped together here to help you choose plants for particular conditions, situations and uses.

plants for fragrance

Fragrance is a real bonus with indoor plants and some of the following have very powerful scents (although some people may consider the smell of hyacinths over-powering). The amount of fragrance these plants produce is usually related to temperature, with scent being stronger in warm rooms. In the case of pelargonium and plectranthus, it is the foliage rather than the flowers that smell, and they release their aroma when the leaves are handled.

- *Cyclamen persicum* (some cvs.)
- *Echinopsis eyriesii*
- *Exacum*
- *Gardenia*
- *Heliotropium*
- *Hoya*
- *Hyacinthus*
- *Jasminum*
- *Miltoniopsis*
- *Narcissus papyraceus*
- *Pelargonium* (scented leaves)
- *Plectranthus* (scented leaves)

Jasminum

plants with long-lived flowers

The long-lived flowers of the following plants make a good alternative to buying bunches of cut blooms, and if treated correctly most will provide a show of flowers the next year too. In plants such as aechmea and justicia the flowers are small and short-lived, but emerge from brightly coloured and persistent bracts.

- *Aechmea*
- *Anthurium*
- *Calathea crocata*
- *Gerbera*
- *Guzmania*
- *Hippeastrum*
- *Justicia*
- *Kalanchoe*
- *Pachystachys*
- *Paphiopedilum*
- *Phalaenopsis*
- *Spathiphyllum*
- *Tillandsia*

plants with decorative foliage

Foliage comes in a huge range of colours and it is possible to have a large collection of plants with scarcely any green in the display. Codiaeum and solenostemon are the gaudiest plants, with reds, pinks, purples and yellows all appearing on the same leaf in some cultivars. Echeveria is available in muted, glaucous pinks and blues.

- *Aglaonema*
- *Codiaeum*
- *Ctenanthe*
- *Echeveria*
- *Gynura*
- *Hypoestes*
- *Iresine*
- *Maranta*
- *Neoregelia*
- *Pilea*
- *Solenostemon*
- *Stromanthe*

plants for temporary colour

These cheap and cheerful pot plants provide a bright focal point for a few weeks and can then be replaced. The majority are flowering but the capsicum and nertera have brilliantly coloured fruits.

- *Begonia* Eliator hybrids
- *Calceolaria*
- *Capsicum*
- *Chrysanthemum*
- *Cyclamen*
- *Exacum*
- *Hyacinthus*
- *Kalanchoe blossfeldiana* hybrids
- *Nertera*
- *Primula*
- *Rhododendron*
- *Saintpaulia*
- *Sinningia*

Chrysanthemum

plants to clean the air

Plants reduce carbon dioxide levels and air temperatures in buildings, as well as raise humidity to create a more pleasant environment. In the 1980s, research by NASA revealed that several species are also capable of removing from the air harmful chemical compounds such as benzene (found in paints and plastics), formaldehyde (in carpets, tissues, fibre board, foam insulation) and trichloroethylene (found in varnishes and adhesives).

- *Chlorophytum*
- *Chrysanthemum*
- *Dracaena*
- *Ficus*
- *Gerbera*
- *Hedera*
- *Nephrolepis*
- *Phoenix*
- *Rhapis*
- *Schefflera*
- *Spathiphyllum*

plants to boost oxygen

Plants breathe in oxygen and give out carbon dioxide, just like humans. But during the day this activity is reversed – plants use the carbon dioxide in the air for photosynthesis and give off oxygen, some at higher levels than others. It makes good sense therefore to surround ourselves with some good oxygenators.

- *Anthurium*
- *Begonia*
- *Calathea*
- *Chlorophytum*
- *Cymbidium*
- *Dracaena*
- *Epipremnum*
- *Guzmania*
- *Monstera*
- *Spathiphyllum*
- *Vriesia*

Monstera

plants for direct sun

Direct sun through window glass can cause problems for many foliage plants, the main symptoms being colour bleached from the leaves and patches of dead tissue appearing. Flowering plants tend to do better than foliage plants in direct sun, and of course cacti and succulents thrive in these conditions.

- *Abutilon*
- *Agave*
- *Aloe*
- *Billbergia*
- *Capsicum*
- *Codiaeum*
- *Crassula*
- *Echeveria*
- *Faucaria*
- *Ferocactus*
- *Iresine*
- *Justicia*
- *Kalanchoe*
- *Nolina*
- *Pelargonium*
- *Solenostemon*
- *Zamioculcas*

large plants

If you have a large, high-ceilinged room you may want to buy a specimen with immediate architectural impact, rather than wait for a small speciment to grow. The plants listed below are often readily available at a height of 1.5m (5ft) or more.

- *Cordyline*
- *Cycas*
- *Dracaena*
- *Euphorbia* (cactus types)
- *Ficus*
- *Jasminum*
- *Monstera*
- *Musa*
- *Nolina*
- palms (most)
- *Philodendron*
- *Schefflera*
- *Yucca*

plants for dark places

No plant can live without light as it is essential for photosynthesis to take place. However, plants native to heavily shaded temperate or tropical forests can be left in a fairly dark corner for many months without suffering too much, especially if watering is kept to a mimimum to slow the growth rate. Periodically switch such plants around so that they all occasionally receive higher levels of light. Variegated plants have less chlorophyll (green pigment) in the leaves and so require a bright position.

- *Aglaonema*
- *Aspidistra*
- *Aucuba*
- *Calathea*
- *Dracaena*
- *Fatsia*
- *Hedera*
- *Peperomia*
- *Philodendron*
- *Pilea*
- *Rhapis*
- *Soleirolia*
- *Spathiphyllum*

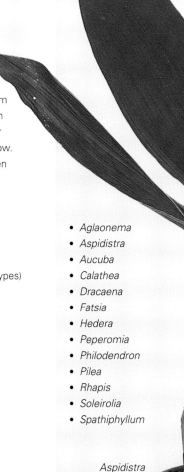

Aspidistra

choosing the best plants/2

plants tolerant of draughts

Most houseplants come from the tropics and will quickly die if situated in a draught, particularly a cold one. However, a few species are sturdy enough to cope with a position by the front door. All those listed here can also be grown in the garden.

- *Aspidistra*
- *Aucuba*
- *Chrysanthemum*
- *Cyclamen*
- *Euonymus*
- *Fatsia*
- *Hedera*
- *Rhododendron*

plants for unheated rooms

Even rooms that get very cold in winter, such as porches, can support a range of plants. The advantage of a cold room is that it encourages flowering plants such as cyclamen, chrysanthemums and azaleas to have an extended blooming period.

- *Araucaria*
- *Aspidistra*
- *Aucuba*
- *Chrysanthemum*
- *Cyclamen*
- *Euonymus*
- *Fatsia*
- *Hedera*
- *Oxalis*
- *Rhododendron*
- *Saxifraga*
- *Solanum*

Cyclamen

plants that thrive in dry air

Humidity levels are affected by temperature, and in most centrally heated rooms the air can be as dry as that in a desert, which can cause the leaf tips of many plants to turn brown. The following species cope better than most with dry air.

- *Agave*
- *Aucuba*
- *Ceropegia*
- *Crassula*
- *Cycas*
- *Dracaena*
- *Echeveria*
- *Echinopsis*
- *Epipremnum*
- *Faucaria*
- *Ferocactus*
- *Haworthia*
- *Kalanchoe*
- *Mammillaria*
- *Opuntia*
- *Radermachera*
- *Sansevieria*
- *Sedum*
- *Senecio*
- *Yucca*

plants to increase humidity

The air inside most buildings is very dry, and this can aggravate minor ailments such as sore eyes and throats. Levels of dust and air-borne allergens are lower where humidity levels are higher. As plants release 97 per cent of the water they take up, foliage plants will contribute to increasing general levels of humidity in the home.

- *Anthurium*
- *Asparagus*
- *Calathea*
- *Chlorophytum*
- *Cymbidium*
- *Cyperus*
- *Fatsia*
- *Monstera*
- *Phalaenopsis*
- *Spathiphyllum*

plants that thrive in humid air

Most popular houseplants are native to tropical forests where the air is very moist, and tend to do well in rooms such as the bathroom, where humidity is higher than average. However, if the plants are over-crowded and air circulation is poor, fungal diseases may be encouraged.

- *Adiantum*
- *Asparagus*
- *Asplenium*
- *Calathea*
- *Columnea*
- *Ctenanthe*
- *Cymbidium*
- *Dieffenbachia*
- *Episcia*
- *Fittonia*
- *Gynura*
- *Hypoestes*
- *Impatiens*
- *Maranta*
- *Miltoniopsis*
- *Musa*
- *Nephrolepis*
- *Pachystachys*
- *Pteris*
- *Saintpaulia*
- *Sinningia*
- *Tillandsia*

Ctenanthe

plants that need lots of water

The following plants are a good choice for anyone who habitually over-waters plants, although only true bog plants such as cyperus and the venus fly trap (*Dionaea*) can cope with standing in saucers of water. Ease off watering in the winter, when the days are shorter and the plants are not in active growth. And bear in mind that over-watering is the biggest killer of houseplants.

- *Calceolaria*
- *Chrysanthemum*
- *Cyperus*
- *Dionaea*
- *Exacum*
- ferns
- *Nertera*
- *Paphiopedilum*
- *Primula*
- *Pteris*
- *Rhododendron*
- *Soleirolia*
- *Spathiphyllum*
- *Tolmiea*

plants that need little water

Cacti and succulents have a remarkable capacity to survive without water for months on end. As a rule they are fairly small plants, but when something with a bit of impact is required try a tall ponytail plant (*Nolina recurvata*). Remember though that no plant can survive in permanently dessicated compost and the growth of even cacti will be improved with occasional moderate watering.

- *Ceropegia*
- *Echinopsis*
- *Euphorbia milii*
- *Euphorbia trigona*
- *Faucaria*
- *Ferocactus*
- *Lithops*
- *Mammillaria*
- *Nolina recurvata*
- *Zamioculcas*

plants that thrive on neglect

If you like the idea of houseplants but are reluctant or unable to spend much time maintaining them, then the following are worth considering. All can go for long periods without water and don't need deadheading, staking, pruning or even annual repotting.

- *Agave*
- *Aglaonema*
- *Aspidistra*
- *Chlorophytum*
- *Cordyline*
- *Crassula*
- *Dracaena*
- *Echinopsis*
- *Ficus*
- *Howea*
- *Haworthia*
- *Mammillaria*
- *Monstera*
- *Nolina*
- *Sansevieria*
- *Yucca*

plants for children

The following plants are either easy to grow and propagate, such as spider plant (*Chlorophytum comosum*), or are fun to have even if they do require a bit more care, such as banana (*Musa*) and venus fly trap (*Dionaea*).

- *Chlorophytum comosum* (easy to propagate)
- *Dionaea* (insectivorous)
- *Eichhornia* (aquatic)
- *Musa* (exotic)
- *Saxifraga* (easy to propagate)
- *Solenostemon* (bright foliage, easy to grow)
- *Tolmiea* (easy to propagate)
- *Tradescantia* (easy to grow and propagate)

Dionaea

Yucca

A touch of creativity will bring out the best in your houseplants. The way they are displayed is fundamental to how they look, so after considering physical needs, think about how and where a plant can show itself off to best advantage. Plastic pots are not objects of beauty, so be on the lookout for attractive containers – ceramic, basketware, metal, glass – that will complement your plants. Or try some of the ideas for decorating pots. Top-dressings of shingle, shells and crystals look pretty, while unusual containers, such as glass bottles or terrariums, make eyecatching displays. For a bit of fun, have a go at cultivating plants from everyday bits and pieces – coffee beans, ginger, apple or lemon pips.

Vriesea carinata

more plant ideas

decorating pots

Containers present you with a great opportunity to show off your artistic talents. There are lots of quick and easy ways to make them look good and entirely individual, enhancing your houseplant and contributing to the decor of your home in much the same way as would a vase or an ornament.

Decorating a plant pot is an ideal way to experiment with creative skills, as it is such a manageable size. After all, if it goes wrong, you can either paint over your efforts or discard it altogether and not much is lost. If it goes well, you will have created a container that enhances both your plant and your home.

coordinating patterns

Choose the colours and patterns for your pot according to the style of the room it will be in. You can either make a pot stand out as a feature, by using a contrasting colour, or blend it into its surroundings by picking up tones and shades from the room's decorative scheme. If you feel adventurous, you could trace part of a fabric design onto a clear acetate film and convert this into a stencil. Or you could personalise a container more simply, by sticking on a decorative label.

plain or patterned?

In a modern interior where simple clean lines and neutral colours prevail, a single large pot in a plain colour, stamped or stencilled with a strong geometric design, can be just the thing to bring a corner of a room to life. For a more traditional room, you could choose pastel tones and apply pretty paint effects such as sponging in complementary colours. Using more than one matching painted pot can be very effective in lifting a group of plain foliaged plants. Flowering plants often look better in quite plainly decorated pots, the exception being spring bulbs, which can carry exuberant designs.

great ways to decorate pots

The effects on this page were achieved quickly and easily – the methods are briefly described below so you can try them out, or invent some of your own (see page 122 for details of materials and information on how you can experiment). All the pots are made of terracotta, except 7 and 8, which are plastic, and 9 which is tin.

1 Sealed, then roughly gilded with metal leaf.
2 Painted in red emulsion, then sponged with gold craft paint.
3 Painted in dark blue emulsion, stickers attached, over-painted in light blue, stickers removed, swirls applied in chinagraph pencil.
4 Wrapped with wide paper string stuck down with PVA, then painted all over in light green emulsion. Gold wax crayon rubbed over the string when dry.
5 Painted in red emulsion outside, black acrylic inside, stencilled with gold craft paint.
6 Roughly sponged in three coats of different but similar colours of emulsion.
7 Sprayed with silver paint, tile stickers attached.
8 Sprayed with gold paint, then sprayed with gold glitter, then spattered with liquid 'Treasure Gold' – a solvent based paint used for gilding.
9 Painted in lilac acrylic, tile stickers attached.
10 Painted in brown emulsion, then glass mosaic tiles stuck on with strong household adhesive.
11 Painted in pink emulsion, coated in PVA, rolled in glitter, sealed with PVA.
12 and **13** Painted in bronze and gold acrylic metallic paints.

4

9

These large pots were painted in household emulsion, in colours that blend with the tone of the carpet. The leaf motif was then applied in a contrasting colour with a ready-made stamp.

12

13

decorating pots/2

special plant pot effects

Jazz up a prepared pot quickly and easily by applying any of the materials below. Most are easily found in craft shops, or DIY stores.

● **paint** Paint is wonderfully versatile and can be applied in a number of ways. It can be brushed on to create a flat coat, sprayed, sponged or ragged onto a surface, splattered in blobs for an uneven texture, or applied through a stencil with a special brush. Acrylic paint is the most useful, and is available in art shops. However, household emulsion paint is basically the same thing, and is much cheaper. You can buy small quantities in colour tester pots in DIY stores, or tins of paint for larger pots. You can also mix them together to create your own colours. Spray paints are often oil-based and should be used with caution,

following the instructions. They are available in a wide variety of finishes and textures, from high gloss or matt to flecked stone and hammered metal.

● **paintbrushes** Use inexpensive household paintbrushes for covering larger areas and artist's brushes for finer work. Special brushes are available for stencilling. All can be washed out in water after use as long as you are using water-based paints such as acrylic and emulsion.

● **sealants** Sealants are sometimes needed to seal the surface before decoration (as with terracotta pots), and again for protecting the finished effect. PVA is good for both purposes. Although it looks milky when you buy it, it dries clear and does not affect the colour underneath. An alternative is acrylic varnish which comes as a spray or liquid in matt, satin or gloss finishes.

decoupage

Cut out the image with very sharp pointed scissors and apply PVA glue, then stick onto the prepared pot. Rub over the image gently with some kitchen paper to remove any air bubbles or excess glue. Seal when completely dry with acrylic varnish. For an antique effect, tint the varnish with a small amount of raw umber acrylic paint.

● **adhesives** Most versatile is PVA; it is waterbased so it can be thinned with a little water to use as a sealant as well. For sticking heavy objects such as tiles, use strong epoxy glue. Glue guns are useful for textiles and ribbons.

pot preparation

For a successful finish, your will need to prepare the surface of your pot.

plastic pots

To make sure the pot is clean and dust-free, wash in warm soapy water, then rinse well and allow to dry. Spray paint will adhere best to this surface, so cover with several coats, applying each coat very thinly, allowing each coat to dry fully first. The pot should not require sealing, unless you apply further decorative effects.

terracotta pots

These porous pots should be absolutely clean and free from dust before decorating. If they have been used, remove all traces of old soil and mossy deposits with a stiff brush. Wash with warm soapy water and rinse well, then

Use an ordinary household paintbrush to seal a terracotta pot inside and out with two coats of PVA before decorating. Wash the brush in running water immediately after use.

leave to dry completely. Before painting, apply a sealant such as ordinary PVA inside and out and allow to dry. Paint on at least two coats of base coat, such as household emulsion or acrylic paint. Even when sealed, planting directly into decorated terracotta may cause the finish to spoil, so it is best to use them as outer pots.

wood pots

To prepare unfinished and previously painted wood, sand down the surface in the direction of the grain and dust

well before applying a primer coat or two of household emulsion. After decorating, seal with a spray varnish or, for a more durable effect, use a polyurethane varnish for sealing wooden floors (although this can sometimes alter the colour of the surface underneath).

metal pots

Remove any traces of rust with fine steel wool. Dust pots with a household paintbrush to remove any residue of steel wool, then wash and dry thoroughly before painting with a base coat. Metal primer should be used for old pots, but it is not vital; household emulsion will also provide a good surface to decorate further. As with wood, metal pots do benefit from sealing after decorating.

- **stickers** Self-adhesive circles and squares are available in stationers, and the metallic stickers used to decorate walls and tiles are found in DIY stores. Press onto the base coat, then paint over the pot in a second colour. Peel off the stickers, then you can either leave the shape left behind in the colour of the base coat, or decorate it with a squiggle drawn in a china marking pencil.

- **stencils and stamps** These are quick and easy techniques, and virtually foolproof once you have practised on scrap paper.

- **metal leaf** Using this requires a bit of practise, but it is easier if you go for a patched effect where the base terracotta shows through. Packs of metal leaf can be found in craft stores and generally come with instructions.

- **pens and pencils** Varieties you can buy are: wax crayons, china markers, artists oil bar, stencil crayon, gold oil pastel and calligraphy felt-tip pens.

- **ribbon and string** You can create a great effect very simply by using ribbons and strings, which are now available in all sorts of widths, materials and colours.

- **glitter** Paint the pot in a base colour, then apply PVA to part of the surface and roll in glitter. Repeat until covered. When dry, spray with acrylic varnish.

- **tiles** Stick glass mosaic tiles, available from craft shops in small packs or from tiling outlets, onto prepared pots with small blobs of strong adhesive. Stick tiles around the rim, or for an all-over mosaic effect, embed them in tile cement spread thickly onto a pot.

- **prints** Buy prints made especially for decoupage from craft shops, or use colour images from magazines. Black and white images look very effective if finished off with a coat of tinted varnish to give an aged effect.

labelling pots

This is a great way to decorate pots of herbs or small cuttings for gifts. First practise writing the name with a paintbrush, or a calligraphy felt tipped pen, on scrap paper. Perhaps the easiest way is to write onto a self-adhesive address label and then stick that onto the pot. Or you can write directly onto the pot. In this case, first write very lightly with a white china marker or soft crayon, then paint over the letters using an artist's brush. If you like you can brush on tinted varnish to 'antique' the finished pot.

painting stripes on a terracotta pot

1 Using household emulsion or artist's acrylic paint, apply a base coat to the prepared pot and allow to dry. Stick masking tape in vertical bands. Press the tape down firmly to achieve a good edge for the stripes.

2 Paint the spaces between the bands of masking tape in contrasting or coordinating colours using a small household paintbrush. To make a checked effect, apply the tape in horizontal bands as well. Pleat the tape where the pot narrows to achieve a sealed edge.

3 Once the paint is dry, carefully remove the tape. It is almost impossible to get a completely clean line as the paint seeps under the tape, but you can use a fine artist's paintbrush to touch up areas. Finish the pot with a coat of acrylic spray varnish.

displaying houseplants

Whether a houseplant is the centre of attention or part of the background decoration in a room depends on how and where it is displayed.

siting your plant

When deciding where to position a plant, first consider the conditions in which that plant grows in the wild, then match these as closely as possible. For example, a woodland floor plant, such as a fern, will not last long on a sunny windowsill. Make sure your plants are in an environment in which they can thrive.

Next, think about the form of a plant. The trailing stems of ivy (*Hedera*) need to tumble over the edge of a shelf or sill and have a softening effect on a room. In contrast, a bushy peperomia or pilea sit pertly upright and complement the shape of a small side table. Be careful, though, if placing plants on good-quality furniture as water spills will damage the finish.

Treat flowering and berrying plants such as cyclamen, grape hyacinths and pineapple lilies as temporary seasonal ornaments and change them as required.

single specimens

For sheer impact, nothing makes a better focal point than a solitary large specimen plant. Its structure can vary from stemless (such as aloe) to single-stemmed (yucca) or multistemmed (*Asparagus setaceus*). Shapely palms and figs work well, as do climbers such as swiss cheese plants trained vertically. Large specimens are best placed on the floor.

A prominently displayed plant needs a suitably impressive container. Most plants are enhanced by a simple pot, although plants with plain dark leaves can look spectacular in a patterned or multicoloured pot, provided this ties in with the style and décor of the room.

If the pot is placed on a stand, this also plays a large part in the look and overall effect. Wooden or metal pot stands are available for multi-pot displays, while individual plants can be supported on almost anything, as long as it complements both pot and plant.

Background and lighting can make all the difference. A plain wall will show a plant to its best advantage – plants can get lost against a 'busy' pattern. Clever use of lighting can enhance an effect – for example, if the light source is placed to cast dramatic shadows. However, light shows up dust, so leaves need to be cleaned regularly to make the difference between a good focal point and a stunning one, and also to encourage healthy growth.

Display plants so that their foliage habit is enhanced. Here, rosary vines (*Ceropegia linearis* subsp. *woodii*) trail down a white wall, while spider plants (*Chlorophytum comosum* 'Vittatum') arch over their baskets.

---

temporary plants
for seasonal flowers

SPRING ● grape hyacinth (*Muscari*)
● *Iris danfordiae* ● *Iris reticulata*
● *Narcissus* ● *Primula*
SUMMER ● *Begonia* ● black sarana
(*Fritillaria camschatcensis*)
● *Capsicum* ● heliotrope
(*Heliotropium*) ● lilies (*Lilium*)
AUTUMN ● autumn crocus (*Colchicum*)
● autumn daffodil (*Sternbergia*)
● *Nerine* ● pineapple lily (*Eucomis autumnalis*) ● winter cherry (*Solanum*)
WINTER ● *Crocus* ● *Cyclamen*
● hyacinth (*Hyacinthus*) ● *Narcissus*
● snowdrop (*Galanthus*)

Vertical stands are useful in confined spaces. Above, top to bottom, are pick-a-back plant (*Tolmiea*), spider plant and kalanchoe. The semicircular wire stand (above left) clearly has room for more than its current display of, from left to right, white phalaenopsis, red trailing aeschynanthus, red miltoniopsis and begonia.

Plants often look best in containers that reflect the natural environment. Left to right: venus fly trap (*Dionaea*), bead plant (*Nertera granadensis*) and mind-your-own-business (*Soleirolia*).

grouping plants

All the plants in a group display should have similar light and temperature requirements (see pages 28 and 30), but they can vary in size, shape, texture and colour. One good combination would be a palm as the specimen plant, accompanied by croton (*Codiaeum*), caladium, dumb cane (*Dieffenbachia*), creeping fig (*Ficus pumila*) and ivy. If there is space, introduce some seasonality by adding temporary plants at different times of the year. In most groupings, matching pots look better than mixed ones.

Displaying plants in a group helps to create a beneficial damp microclimate around them. This counters the common problem of over-dry air in the house, which is a major cause of plant failure. To increase humidity (see also page 32), stand the pots on a large tray filled with ornamental chippings or gravel. Top up the tray with water, which will evaporate to keep the air moist around the plants. Make sure the pot bases stand on the gravel and not in the water, otherwise the compost will become waterlogged and the plants will suffer or even die.

plant window

A double-glazed window with a wide sill can be converted into a plant window by adding sliding glass doors to the inside of the reveal. This forms, in effect, a terrarium (see page 132). The window should receive either early morning or late afternoon sun, so the plants do not burn. Plants will flourish provided they are kept healthy and carefully watered. Bromeliads are particularly suited to this environment.

displaying multiplanted pots

A group of houseplants can be successfully grown together in a single bowl to create a miniature indoor garden. As the plants share the same potting compost, their wellbeing depends on enjoying the same conditions, not only of light and temperature (see pages 28 and 30) but also humidity and watering (see page 32).

mix and match

An indoor garden can range from a modestly planted bowl to a spectacular display in a purpose-built container, but whatever its scale it is essential that you match the individual requirements of the plants you plan to include. For example, you can put azalea and cyperus together, as they both like very moist, preferably acid, compost, but you would be ill-advised to add a peperomia, because it prefers drier conditions and would most likely rot in such a situation.

A basic planting arrangement suitable for most containers is one large specimen with a mix of smaller foliage plants, varying in shape, habit and texture. Try to include some permanent plants that produce seasonal floral displays and one or more trailing foliage plants to soften the edge. Then, if you like, add temporary flowering plants in season (see page 124).

containers

Containers can range from wide ceramic bowls to wooden troughs lined with polythene or similar water-retaining material (see also page 26). A purpose-built raised brick bed is even possible in a conservatory or sunroom. Whatever the container, adequate drainage is vital, either through holes in the base to a drip tray, or by placing drainage materials over the base before filling the container with potting compost (see page 43).

A plain container usually works best for a multiplanted design, as it allows the plants to provide the main decorative feature. The pot could be decorated to blend with its surroundings by using one of the many plant-safe paints and wood stains available.

garden styles

These are some traditional indoor garden styles that depend on a particular type of container or mix of plants.

permanent plants
with seasonal flowers

SPRING ● *Anthurium* ● *Camellia* ● *Jasminum polyanthum* ● african violet (*Saintpaulia*)
SUMMER ● *Abutilon* ● *Begonia* ● *Bougainvillea* ● peace lily (*Spathiphyllum*) ● *Pelargonium* (regal cvs.) ● *Rosa* ● rose of china (*Hibiscus rosa-sinensis*) ● *Streptocarpus*
AUTUMN ● *Cymbidium* ● *Justicia* ● *Kalanchoe*
WINTER ● azalea (*Rhododendron simsii*) ● poinsettia (*Euphorbia pulcherrima*)

Abutilon megapotamicum

The white anthurium flowers light up this indoor garden, their colours echoed by the variegated peperomia at the front. The soft fronds of *Blechnum gibbum* and trails of plain green ivy add excellent textural variation.

● **dish gardens** usually comprise cacti and other succulents growing in a pan covered with coarse grit or pea gravel, perhaps with one or two rocks added. These can look superb in summer, when the plants flower, and they also provide interest during winter.

● **pots-et-fleur** combine a permanent plant display, usually mainly foliage, with a small number of temporary, seasonal cut flowers (right). The cut flowers are placed in a narrow vase or florists' tube that has been sunk into the potting compost as part of the planting arrangement.

● **miniature gardens** usually have an oriental theme. A pan is minimally planted with bonsai (see page 138), short decorative grasses and mosses, between which wind little paths. Small ornaments, buildings or figurines are added to create a landscape in miniature. As the plants are usually hardy, the garden can be kept in an unheated conservatory for most of the year, and placed outside for the summer.

● **suspended gardens** are an excellent way to display trailing plants and those that produce plantlets at the end of

pots-et-fleur

1 **Place drainage material** in a bowl. Set a vase in the centre and then partially fill around the vase with fresh potting compost. Plant up with hypoestes and *Asparagus densiflorus.*

2 **Finish planting up the bowl** with another colour variant of hypoestes, and carefully water the plants in. Fill the central vase with water and add seasonal cut flowers, such as roses.

stems, such as spider plants. Individual pots can be suspended in hangers made, for example, of ceramic, macramé or threaded shells. Always keep a saucer under the pot to avoid damaging the floor covering with water drips.

Alternatively, grow a selection of plants in a hanging basket, which is best hung from a conservatory roof, where plants have good all-round light. A solid basket with a built-in drip tray stops the water dripping on the floor.

evergreen plants
for suspended gardens

● asparagus fern (*Asparagus densiflorus* Sprengeri Group) ● *Begonia* (trailing tuberous sp.) ● creeping fig (*Ficus pumila*) ● ivy (*Hedera*) ● *Philodendron* ● pick-a-back plant (*Tolmiea*) ● *Plectranthus* ● prayer plant (Maranta) ● spider plant (*Chlorophytum comosum*) ● *Tradescantia*

planting a hanging basket

1 **Place the hanging basket** on a bucket or wide pot, for stability. Cover the basket base with a layer of lightweight drainage material. Add soil-less potting compost and firm gently.

2 **Arrange trailing plants** such as ivy around the edge to cover the rim of the basket. Pack more compost around their rootballs so there are no air gaps, and firm gently into place.

3 **Place bushy plants** in the centre (here impatiens and begonia), and top up with compost, leaving about 1cm (½in) at the top to allow for watering. Firm well and then water thoroughly.

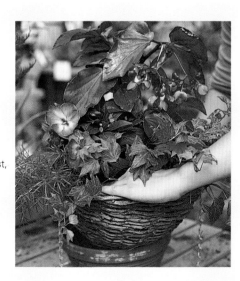

year-round scent

A succession of flowering houseplants can contribute natural perfume through the seasons, making it a pleasure to enter a room. There is a fragrance to suit every mood, as scents range from light and fresh to strong and heady.

Jasmine is best in a porch or hall, where its strong perfume in summer will be appreciated by anyone walking by.

It is tempting to fill your home with a variety of different scents, but bear in mind that appreciation of perfume is highly subjective, and what might be pleasing to one person can be offensive to another. The intensity of a fragrance varies according to the plant and the conditions and situation in which it is kept. Plants such as narcissus, lily-of-the-valley and primulas produce a light perfume suitable for a living room or bedroom during winter. Later on in the year, you may find the scents of miniature roses, lilies and orchids more appealing – some of the miniature cymbidiums have a particularly delicate scent. Citrus flowers have a strong but not overpowering fragrance, and often appear throughout the year if the plant is in good light.

Smell a miniature rose before you buy. Some varieties have highly fragrant flowers, while the perfume of others can be subtle or even non-existent.

Gardenias exude a beguiling fragrance. Once widely used for table decorations, buttonholes and corsages, they are seen less often nowadays, having gained a reputation for being 'difficult'. But to flower reliably all they need is even temperature and high levels of humidity; it is draughts and dryness that cause them to drop their buds, so position them in a sheltered spot rather than in a hall or other draughty area.

Myrtle and its variegated cultivars are neat, scented evergreen shrubs that bloom from July to September. They are not fully hardy, so bring them indoors when the buds start to open and keep them in the house or greenhouse until the following May.

In a porch, hall or conservatory, you might enjoy a more powerful perfume, especially during the evening. Plants such as *Hoya lanceolata* subsp. *bella*, jasmine and stephanotis give off intoxicating fragrances. These climbing houseplants flower best in bright all-round light. Another plant well worth considering is the slightly tender evergreen star jasmine and its variegated forms, which can be grown permanently indoors if summer shading is provided. Their heavily scented flowers open in summer and perfume a room all day long.

Some plants are worth including in the living room for their aromatic foliage. Scented-leaved pelargoniums are an excellent choice for a well-lit spot, where they will give off their distinct fragrances, ranging from rose to mint, orange or lemon.

On a kitchen windowsill, pots of favourite culinary herbs, such as basil, thyme and parsley (see page 146), will grow for short periods, providing a slight aroma if touched.

forcing flowers for winter and spring

Some of the most beautifully fragrant bulbs and shrubs flower outdoors in late winter and early spring, but there is no reason why you cannot enjoy them indoors too. Seasonal bulbs such as strong but sweetly scented hyacinths and paper-white narcissus provide great sensual pleasure when forced into early

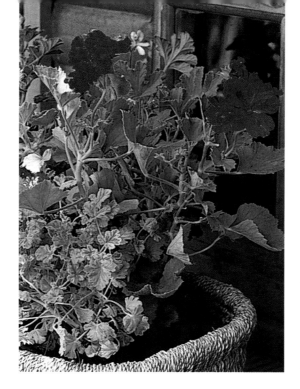

The scented-leaved pelargonium at the front of this pot gives off its aroma most strongly when a leaf is touched. The blooms are modest, so for extra colour a flowering but unscented regal pelargonium is planted alongside.

flower indoors for Christmas or early in the new year (see page 46).

Alternatively, you can try a technique that was popular in Victorian and Edwardian times as a means of enjoying early scented blossom in the house. Grow small fragrant-flowered shrubs in pots outside through the summer, watering and feeding them regularly. At the end of October move the potted shrubs inside to a cool, well-lit hall, glazed porch or conservatory,

where they will blossom earlier than normal. Return them to the garden after flowering to recover, preferably from mid-May onwards when there is little risk of frost (overwintering indoors makes the foliage more tender than normal). You could stand the shrubs in a greenhouse if you have one.

One of the best shrubs for forcing in this way is *Daphne odora* 'Aureomarginata', an evergreen with gold-margined leaves. It usually flowers in March but will bloom much earlier indoors. Even stronger fragrance emanates from *Daphne mezereum*; its flowers will appear on bare branches for New Year.

fragrant houseplants for every season

SPRING ● *Citrus* ● *Cyclamen* (some) ● *Cytisus* x *spachianus* ● *Daphne* (forced, some) ● *Freesia* (some) ● *Gardenia* ● hedge wattle (*Acacia paradoxa*) ● herbs ● *Hyacinthus* ● *Jasminum polyanthum* ● lily-of-the-valley (*Convallaria majalis*) ● mimosa (*Acacia dealbata*) ● *Narcissus* (some) ● orchids (some) ● rose bay (*Nerium oleander*) ● *Stephanotis* ● *Viburnum* x *burkwoodii* (forced)

SUMMER ● angels' trumpets (*Brugmansia*, some) ● *Bouvardia longiflora* ● *Citrus* ● *Coelogyne cristata* ● *Cymbidium* (some miniature hybrids) ● frangipani (*Plumeria*) ● *Gardenia* ● *Heliotropium* ● herbs ● lilies (*Lilium*,

some) ● myrtle (*Myrtus communis*) ● pinks (*Dianthus*, some) ● *Rosa* (some) ● rose bay (*Nerium oleander*) ● star jasmine (*Trachelospermum jasminoides*) ● *Stephanotis* ● wax flower (*Hoya*)

AUTUMN ● *Bouvardia longiflora* ● *Citrus* ● *Gardenia* ● herbs ● myrtle (*Myrtus communis*) ● *Pelargonium* (scented-leaved) ● *Stephanotis*

WINTER ● *Citrus* ● *Cyclamen persicum* (some) ● *Daphne* (forced, some) ● herbs ● *Hyacinthus* (forced) ● *Jasminum polyanthum* (forced) ● mimosa (*Acacia dealbata*) ● paper-white narcissus (*Narcissus papyraceus*) ● *Pelargonium* (scented-leaved) ● *Primula* (forced, some)

Gardenia jasminoides

● tasmanian blue gum (*Eucalyptus globulus*)

bromeliads & air plants

Bromeliads are a distinctive group of tropical houseplants that are usually grown for their stunning leaf colour and long-lasting, spectacular flower spikes. The extraordinary air plants are a fascinating novelty.

In their native American jungle, bromeliads grow on trees or the forest floor, obtaining moisture and the small amount of nutrients they need either from the humid atmosphere or the rainwater that collects on their foliage or in a central 'vase'. As their style of growth is so different to most other houseplants, these tree dwellers grow best when displayed in as natural a setting as possible.

Bromeliads can be used as eye-catching specimens or integrated with more conventional houseplants to add foliage interest and flower colour. Aechmea, billbergia, guzmania and vriesea are varieties cultivated specifically for their flowers. Most bromeliads do not require soil as a source of nutrients or water, but use it only as an anchor. This means that they can be attached to a rock or dead branch to form a bromeliad 'tree'. The sculptural qualities of arrangements like these look particularly good in sparse, modern interiors, providing an interesting alternative to a flowering houseplant as a Christmas gift.

Some bromeliads, such as this aechmea, have leaves that naturally form a central 'vase'. They are watered directly into the 'vase', which should be regularly topped up. Avoid watering the compost, because the base of the plant will rot if it gets too wet. Completely empty and refill the 'vase' every two months. These plants benefit from a tiny drop of liquid houseplant fertiliser in the water about once a month in spring and summer.

displaying air plants

YOU WILL NEED • driftwood or an interestingly shaped dead branch • grey tillandsias • air plant adhesive, string or thin plastic-coated wire • mister

1 Thoroughly scrub the driftwood clean and allow to dry. Clear away any compost from the roots of the air plants. Then attach the plants to the branch with glue or string, or wire them into place.

2 Once all the air plants are secured, carefully mist each one. Position the driftwood display in a room with a minimum temperature of 10°C (50°F). Repeat the misting daily.

Some bromeliads are distinguished by the way in which their rosetted leaves form a central 'vase', as for example, in aechmea, guzmania, nidularium and vriesea. These so-called vase plants make excellent specimen houseplants.

Bromeliads are sometimes referred to as 'air plants', but true air plants – the grey tillandsias – differ from other bromeliads in that their leaves are covered with grey furry scales, which are capable of absorbing all the required nutrients and moisture when growing in a humid atmosphere. The most popular are *Tillandsia caput-medusae*, *T. ionantha* and spanish moss (*T. usneoides*). Other species such as *T. juncea*, with its long rush-like leaves, and *T. argentea*, with its untidy mop of silvery hair, can be obtained from specialist nurseries. Air plants are displayed by mounting them on a surface such as driftwood (left), coral, rock or slate.

When growing guzmania, try to provide a warm, humid, well-lit environment, to recreate a sense of its natural habitat in the Andean rainforest.

growing conditions

For success with bromeliads you need to mimic the humid conditions they encounter in the wild. Most need good light with occasional exposure to bright sunshine. A room temperature of 15–21°C (60–70°F) is preferable, although some bromeliads need a hotter environment, about 24°C (75°F), to stimulate flowering.

They all require an extremely well-drained planting medium, so grow them in a mixture of equal quantities by volume of soil-less potting compost and vermiculite.

Because of their watering methods, it is advisable to place all bromeliads – particularly those anchored to a material other than compost – on a surface not likely to be damaged if it becomes wet. Marble, tiles and glass are ideal. Vase plants, such as aechmea, need to be positioned where the 'vase' can be conveniently and accurately topped up with water (above left). Bromeliads that are watered by misting the leaves daily, such as billbergia and tillandsia, benefit from being surrounded by other plants, which help to increase humidity around them.

Vase plants tend to become top-heavy, because the compost serves only as anchorage and not as a source of nutrients. To ensure they are reliably stable, stand their pots in a larger outer container and fill the gap with pebbles.

Soft water is best for bromeliads (here, tillandsia and *Guzmania lingulata*), so if you live in a hard-water area where lime-scale is a problem, use rainwater or cooled boiled tap water (never use water from a water-softener as the chemicals will damage the plant). About once a month during spring and summer, add half-strength liquid houseplant fertiliser to the daily spraying routine.

gardens under glass

Many houseplants originating in humid climates suffer in the dry atmosphere of a centrally heated home. Growing plants within the controlled environment of an enclosed glass container can overcome the problem whilst creating a year-round indoor garden feature.

Gardening under glass is a popular way to grow moisture-loving houseplants, which thrive in the microclimate created inside. Any suitable glass container – a winemaker's demijohn, a goldfish bowl, a deep jar or even a big whisky bottle – will do if properly planted up and maintained. Or you may prefer a terrarium, which is essentially a decorative indoor mini-greenhouse, enabling you to display a larger range of small plants than an open top jar (far right).

Purpose-made terrariums and other glass containers are available in a range of sizes and styles. Ideally, they should be as large as possible, with clear glass (green-tinted glass has an adverse effect on light levels and consequently on plant growth and health) and a large opening for ease of planting.

Before planting, wash the container inside and out with a weak solution of household bleach and water. Rinse thoroughly and allow to dry.

If it is impossible to get your hand inside the container to plant or to level the compost, there are special long-handled tools available, which can be inserted through the bottle neck or door of the container. Most are based on table knives, forks and spoons; you can easily make them yourself by tying these utensils to a short cane.

choosing the plants

The plants that will flourish in a bottle garden are those that require high humidity, such as ferns and bromeliads. Ferns in fact grow considerably better in a covered container than in normal room conditions.

Select suitably sized, slow-growing, ornamental varieties, so they make maximum impact but will not outgrow their environment too soon. Avoid plants such as cacti and succulents as they will rot in damp air. Dead petals on flowering plants need to be removed promptly, so you may prefer to steer clear of these plants, too.

Try to strike a balance between upright, compact and trailing plants, and include a variety of different foliage colours and textures. Position taller plants in the centre, unless the bottle is to be viewed from one side only, in which case place them towards the back. The average bottle garden will hold three to six young plants, and a terrarium eight to ten plants.

plants **for glass gardens**
- bromeliads • creeping fig (*Ficus pumila*) • cretan brake fern (*Pteris cretica*)
- *Dracaena sanderiana*
- earth star (*Cryptanthus*)
- maidenhair fern (*Adiantum*) • painted net leaf (*Fittonia*; right)
- orchids • prayer plant (*Maranta*) • *Selaginella*

In summer, move your terrarium out of the sun. If it is exposed to direct sunlight, temperatures inside will build up to levels that will damage the plants – here *Dracaena sanderiana*, bead plants (*Nertera granadensis*) and a juvenile palm.

1 **Cover the base** with a 2.5cm (1in) drainage layer of washed pea gravel or granite chippings, pouring it in through a cardboard tube or rolled-up paper funnel to avoid damaging the glass. Using the funnel again, cover the drainage material with moist bulb fibre, or a thin layer of charcoal followed by moist multipurpose potting compost.

2 **Before planting,** water the houseplants. Remove one from its pot, tease out the roots, then insert it (here, *Dracaena sanderiana*) in the jar, using a table fork or spoon tied to a cane as a long-handled planting tool.

3 **Carefully firm** the potting compost around the plant roots and stem with a cork attached to the end of a long cane. Continue planting the remaining plants, spacing them 8–10cm (3–4in) apart.

4 **Once planting is complete,** lightly mist the foliage and compost with water. Then leave the plants to settle for a week before misting again.

growing conditions

To thrive, bottle gardens need to be in a well-lit position, but not in full sunlight. This is particularly important in summer, otherwise the plants will 'cook'. Room temperature should be at least 15°C (60°F), as cold, stagnant air within the container can give fungal diseases a chance to take hold. Where the plants are in a closed environment, there is no need to worry about draughts.

Plants should be thoroughly watered before they are planted into moist bulb fibre or other potting compost. Immediately after planting, and again about a week later, if necessary, use a hand sprayer to give just enough water to ensure that the compost is damp but not wet. Then close the terrarium door or cork the glass bottle.

In theory, a sealed terrarium or bottle garden should never need watering again as the plants recycle the available moisture, but it is advisable to check occasionally. An uncorked bottle or jar will need watering from time to time.

If, after the bottle has been corked, condensation forms on the glass, remove the stopper to allow the excess moisture to evaporate before sealing again. You may have to do this several times before you get the amount of moisture in the bottle garden just right. Once the moisture balance is correct, bottle gardens require very little attention, but add a drop of a liquid houseplant fertiliser to the water if and when watering is necessary.

terrariums

With a hinged side for planting, or a removable pane of glass, a terrarium is a convenient receptable for a garden under glass and is easier to tend than those in narrow-necked containers. Purpose-made models often resemble miniature Victorian greenhouses and may be large, elaborate affairs with soldered or leaded glass panels and other embellishments. Unless the structure is properly sealed, however, it will not be self-maintaining. A mirrored back will visually increase the size of the terrarium and reflect light, which will encourage more balanced plant growth. You can make a terrarium from an old fish tank; seal the top with a pane of glass.

Always remove any dying foliage or flowers before they start to rot, using a large pair of scissors for extra reach.

orchids

With their amazing flowers and often flamboyant colour combinations, orchids are like no other plants. Many have very exacting requirements but new, easier hybrids have been developed that are long flowering and suitable for growing indoors.

The easiest orchids to grow as houseplants are the tropical ones, such as the phalaenopsis hybrids, which send up flower shoots almost throughout the year. Almost as prolific are the cymbidiums, especially the many compact hybrids. Others you may see offered by specialist nurseries, garden centres and on orchid stands at garden shows are slipper orchids (*Paphiopedilum*), dendrobiums, pansy orchids (*Miltoniopsis*), oncidiums and scented coelogynes. As long as you follow the cultivation instructions here or on the plant label, or take the advice of the grower, all these orchids should thrive indoors.

displaying orchids

Because the flowers are so spectacular, some orchids look good in simple containers such as white ceramic or metal pots. The plants associate particularly well with the feathery foliage of ferns, which share similar humidity needs. Orchids also thrive in terrariums (see page 133) and plant windows (see page 125), where there is full control of growing conditions.

When flower buds have formed sufficiently to reveal their colouring, move the pot into a decorative potholder whose design and hues complement that of the flowers.

Orchids are not particularly attractive out of flower, so it is important to encourage at least one or two of the plants in a collection to bloom at the same time, unless they are grouped with other types of plant.

Dendrobiums need moderate watering and plenty of indirect light to produce their long-lasting flower stems.

repotting an orchid

1 Remove any flower stems which have flowered at the base, and water the plant (here phalaenopsis). Prepare the new pot by placing a 4cm (1½in) layer of broken pottery crocks in the base. Half-fill the pot with fresh orchid compost. Carefully remove the orchid from its container and gently tease the old compost from the roots. If needed, divide the rootstock and remove any back bulbs, especially in the case of cymbidiums.

2 Prune any dead and damaged roots. Position the orchid in the new pot, at its previous planting level, and work more orchid compost carefully around the roots. Water to settle the compost, and top up with more if necessary. Stand in a shady place for a fortnight while the orchid gets established in its new container. Then move into bright indirect light.

growing conditions

The main cultural needs for orchids are correct compost and the right levels of humidity and light. Most tropical orchids that grow well indoors require a draught-free environment.

● **potting compost** It is important to use special orchid compost, which is designed for free drainage. To improve moisture retention, chopped sphagnum moss can be added.

● **humidity** Many orchids need high humidity, so humidity levels may need to be raised in a warm house or during dry conditions. To do this, group orchids with other houseplants, because the massed foliage will create the extra humidity. Alternatively, place the orchids together on a tray of pebbles kept constantly damp.(see also page 96).

● **light** Most orchids need bright indirect light. The ideal position is close to a sunny window where the sun is filtered by gauze curtains. In a conservatory, fit net or muslin screens to the roof and windows to protect the leaves and flowers from scorching.

Use the measuring spoon that comes with the orchid fertiliser so the exact amount of powder feed is dissolved in the specified volume of water. Then pour some of the solution onto the potting compost.

Although orchids sold as houseplants will, in theory, flower throughout the year, they require 10–15 hours of daylight to do so. In winter, you can supplement natural light with special lamps that reproduce natural daylight (see page 28).

orchid care

Water the top of the compost, with rainwater if possible, and allow the excess water to drain away. Remember these plants often grow on trees where there is perfect drainage. Allow the compost to dry out between watering.

During spring and summer, orchids benefit from feeding with an orchid feed (below) or a houseplant food diluted to quarter strength.

Repotting is needed if an orchid has outgrown its container or when the bark and moss in the compost has started to degrade. It is best to repot in spring, when the plant is in active growth (above). Use a pot 2–5cm (1–2in) larger than the previous one, to allow for growth, but do not use one that is too large, as this can easily result in the orchid receiving too much water.

Phalaenopsis produces flower stems at any time of the year, either from the base of the plant or as side branches off the old flower stem.

indoor water gardens

A wide variety of indoor water features is available nowadays, ranging from simple fountains that can be planted up with an interesting mix of plants, to ambitious sunken ponds designed for large conservatories.

A cascading water feature will raise the humidity level indoors to the benefit of all your houseplants.

For best results, an indoor water garden should be in bright light at all times, ensuring optimum health for its plants. The ideal place is a spacious, sunny conservatory, or a large enclosed porch, preferably with a clear or translucent roof, and good ventilation even during winter. A water garden or feature should be set on a solid floor at or slightly below ground level, so its weight is not a problem. Other factors to bear in mind when choosing a suitable site for your indoor water garden are:

- **access to water** Ideally, there should be a tap close by, because the water will need topping up regularly, especially if a pump is installed. The pump will be damaged if too much water has evaporated.
- **access to electricity** You will need a supply nearby if you plan to install electrically powered features such as a water filter (to break down and purify waste products and noxious gases), a pump for operating a cascade or a small fountain, or other accessories such as underwater lighting.

water safety

Water and electricity are a potentially lethal combination. Make sure you unplug all appliances before carrying out any maintenance work. Also, be careful not to leave cables where they can be tripped over.

choosing plants

To keep the water clear, it is important to use a mixture of marginal (shallow-water) plants, deep-water plants, floating aquatic plants (which prevent the buildup of algae) and submerged oxygenating plants (which absorb minerals and carbon dioxide in the water). If you have a fountain, however, this will do the job of the oxygenators.

Select plants that are suited to the higher air and water temperatures experienced indoors (see below), as those used in outdoor ponds will soon grow tall, lank and unattractive, with few flowers. Don't be tempted

good plants for an indoor water garden

MARGINAL PLANTS ● arum lily (*Zantedeschia aethiopica*)
● *Carex morrowii* 'Variegata'
● *Cyperus albostriatus* ● papyrus (*Cyperus papyrus* 'Nanus')
● umbrella plant (*Cyperus involucratus*) ● variegated japanese rush (*Acorus gramineus* 'Variegatus')
DEEP-WATER PLANTS ● water lilies such as *Nymphaea mexicana* and

N. odorata var. *minor*
TENDER FLOATING AQUATICS ● water chestnut (*Trapa*) ● water hyacinth (*Eichhornia crassipes*) ● water lettuce (*Pistia stratiotes*)
SUBMERGED OXYGENATORS ● curled pondweed (*Potamogeton crispus*)
● curly water thyme (*Lagarosiphon major*) ● milfoil (*Myriophyllum*)

To prevent the soil drifting away in the water garden, line each planting basket with geotextile or hessian, and top-dress the soil with a layer of coarse gravel.

to over-plant; young specimens will grow much quicker indoors than outside, and it is important not to allow any one type of plant to obscure the surface of the water.

You can buy suitable plants from aquarium specialists, by mail order or over the internet. On arrival, always check plants for pests such as whitefly, greenfly and water snails. If infected return them, or treat them and make sure they are pest-free before planting.

Where space allows, the indoor water garden is the perfect place to grow the white arum lily *Zantedeschia aethiopica*. Other suitable marginals are variegated japanese rush, which is often sold as a houseplant but thrives best if the roots are kept constantly wet, and *Carex morrowii* 'Variegata', a sedge that tolerates a wide range of temperatures and prefers its feet in water. Also try spike moss (*Selaginella kraussiana*), a fern-like plant that combines well with most other marginals.

Many tender water lilies produce flowers and leaves that are too large for an average-sized indoor water garden, but there are some varieties of these deep-water plants suitable for a smaller feature, too (see opposite). Water hyacinth is another good candidate for the indoor water garden.

Floating aquatic plants such as water lettuce and water chestnut are widely available, as are oxygenating plants such as curled pondweed, milfoil and curly water thyme.

suitable containers

Indoor water gardens can be created in a variety of containers. Half-barrels, pots, troughs and rigid pre-formed pond units made of wood, terracotta, plastic, fibreglass or hypertufa are all suitable. Check that the container is watertight before planting it up. If necessary, paint the inside with a suitable water sealant or line it with polythene.

Water gardens should have planting shelves so that both marginal and deep-water plants can be grown at their appropriate depths. Alternatively, the plants can be placed on brick stacks.

planting a water garden

The best time to do this is in spring and summer. All plants should be planted in rigid plastic-mesh planting baskets lined with geotextile or hessian, filled with aquatic compost and topped with gravel. These baskets come in a variety of sizes and allow the free movement of water and gases around plant roots.

Make sure that the shoots of young deep-water plants and floating acquatics can reach the surface of the water, even if you have to prop up the plants temporarily. Established plants usually need dividing every spring.

making an indoor water garden

YOU WILL NEED • enough pebbles to cover the base of the container and disguise the pump • waterproof container • submersible pump • selection of water plants, planted in baskets if appropriate • stones, bricks or other supports as necessary

1 **Thoroughly wash** the pebbles to remove any dust and grime, before placing them carefully in the waterproof container around the pump to disguise it.

2 **Two-thirds fill the container** with water and leave to settle. Gently lower each planting basket of marginal or deep-water plants and floating aquatics into the container until only their foliage is on the water's surface.

3 **Support the deep-water** and floating plants (here, water hyacinth and water lettuce) in position with their leaves floating on the water surface, using stones or bricks to give height as necessary. Place submerged oxygenators on the bottom of the water garden. When all the plants have been positioned, top up the water level to within 5cm (2in) of the container's rim. Adjust plant support heights, if necessary. Switch on the pump.

indoor bonsai

Originating in the Far East, bonsai is a method of training and pruning a young tree so that ultimately it resembles a gnarled and aged specimen in miniature. This form of horticultural art is an increasingly popular way to grow trees indoors.

For success with indoor bonsai, it is important to match the needs of the species with the conditions you can provide in your home. Choose tropical and sub-tropical evergreen trees, such as *Serissa foetida*, as they are used to the year-round high temperatures that are found in most houses. Hardier species, such as chinese elm (*Ulmus parvifolia*), also do well, provided they have a summer holiday outdoors. Avoid native and other outdoor hardy trees, such as scots pines (*Pinus sylvestris*) and maples (*Acer*), because they grow poorly indoors, becoming soft and lanky.

Trees can be bought partly trained from garden centres, specialist bonsai nurseries or at shows, or as untrained seedlings from specialist growers. They can be displayed individually, as a group of trees in one container or as a raft planting (that is, with the trunk trained horizontally so the side branches become the upright stems). Bonsai can also be grown on, in or over rocks such as tufa (volcanic rock).

growing conditions

● **light** Bonsai needs constant bright light, so place the plant on a sunny windowsill. As it is difficult to achieve this consistency of light in winter, you may need to supplement the daylight with special growing lights, which are available from garden centres. Bonsai trees will benefit from being put outside in summer in a sunny, sheltered spot.

● **temperature** In winter, keep bonsai plants away from windowsills and direct sources of heat such as radiators. During these months, if they are showing no signs of growth, a minimum temperature of 10°C (50°F) will be fine. During the growing season, most bonsai requires temperatures of 15–21°C (60–70°F).

● **bonsai containers** These should have one or more drainage holes in the bottom, and may also have some small holes for tying the tree in place.

● **potting compost** Plant bonsai in bonsai mix, or in equal quantities of sand and moss peat, which will hold just enough water and yet be free draining.

● **watering and humidity** Bonsai must be kept constantly moist, especially in the growing season,

While outdoor bonsai has been practised for about a thousand years, indoor bonsai is a more recent art, using trees that can be kept indoors for most of the year.

bonsai shapes

There are several basic shapes in which to train a bonsai seedling, some of which are shown here. The process may take up to five years before the tree starts to resemble traditional bonsai styles.

Windswept as this *Juniperus chinensis*

root pruning

1 In early to mid-spring, remove the bonsai (here podocarpus) from its pot. Carefully, tease out the roots using a fork.

2 Cut away the bottom one-third of the root system, including taproot. Then repot the tree in fresh compost mix, working it among the roots.

but must never stand in water. This would block the air flow through the compost and so jeopardise the health of the plants. In winter, mist them to counteract the drying effect of any central heating, or raise humidity in some other way (see page 32). Mist plants in the morning, to discourage diseases such as mildew.

• **fertiliser** Feed with a balanced fertiliser every 3–4 weeks from mid-spring to early autumn. Use a high-potash feed from mid-autumn to mid-winter. Apply no fertiliser from mid-winter to mid-spring.

training bonsai

Decide which basic shape you want to adopt for your seedling bonsai. For the first year, try to shape the plant as much as possible by pruning. Cut back the main stem just above a fat, healthy bud that faces the direction in which you want a branch to develop, or pinch out the growing tip when the stem has reached the required height. Remove some of the lower shoots, cutting back to the main stem, and pinch back the others to encourage bushy growth.

The direction of the

wiring a bonsai tree

Bonsai seedlings can be trained to a specific shape using aluminium bonsai wire, which ranges in gauge from 1mm to 6mm (1/25–1/4in). Choose a gauge appropriate to the thickness of the stem being wired. At the start of the growing season, wind the wire securely enough around the stem to hold it at the angle to which the stem is to be trained, but not so tightly that it constricts growth. Anchor one end of the wire in the compost mix or around the main stem, and avoid covering buds. Always remove the wire within six months.

branches can also be encouraged into the desired shape by wiring them (see above). For example, in the young specimen of *Tsuga canadensis* (below), the branches have been wired to grow downwards.

In the second and subsequent years, prune the tree roots (above left) and repot your bonsai in fresh compost. Pinch out, prune and train the tree annually as new growth is produced.

Formal upright
as this *Juniperus chinensis* 'Blaauw'

Weeping
as this *Tsuga canadensis*

Informal upright
as this *Ficus* species

Slanting
as this *Ulmus parvifolia*

cacti & succulents

Cacti and succulents have undergone a recent renaissance in popularity. Their strong shapes, subtle colouring and easy care make them the ideal living sculptures for a stylish centrally heated home or conservatory.

succulent or cacti?

Both cacti and succulents are fleshy plants, able to store comparatively large amounts of water and so capable of thriving in arid conditions. Cacti differ from other succulents in that they have areoles, which produce spines, bristles, hooks or hairs on swollen stems and, usually, bear no leaves.

● **succulents** often have fleshy leaves, usually in rosettes, with or without a defined stem. Typical succulents suitable as houseplants include aloe, crassula and echeveria. Some of the most distinctive succulents are lithops, commonly known as living stones. These curiosities mimic the stony conditions in which they are found naturally.

Many succulents will not tolerate very hot sunny positions, and in summer prefer an east-facing windowsill or a conservatory that is in shade after midday. If this is not possible, you can move succulents

a cactus garden

YOU WILL NEED • pan or shallow bowl with drainage holes • pea gravel or finely crumbled polystyrene sheeting • cactus compost • selection of desert cacti • coarse grit or fine chippings • strip of cardboard or folded paper

1 Place a 2.5cm (1in) layer of drainage material, such as pea gravel or crumbled polystyrene, in a clean bowl. Top with cactus compost to within 2cm (¾in) of the bowl rim. Remove each cacti from its pot, holding it in a loop of thin card or folded paper to protect your hands.

2 Arrange the cacti in the bowl. Then trickle in more compost round them until the rootballs are buried. Water well, then allow to drain. Top-dress by scooping coarse grit, pea gravel or fine chippings onto the compost surface.

This spiny desert garden (right) is planted with opuntia, echinocactus, mammillaria and cephalocereus.

outdoors during summer, to a spot that catches the morning sun. Succulents prefer at least 10°C (50°F), although they will tolerate temperatures down to 4°C (40°F) in winter.

● **desert cacti** have swollen stems and spines, or a coarse wool-like covering. Typical desert cacti are echinopsis and

Move cacti and succulents outside for a summer 'holiday', plunging their pots into a gritty mix. Here, the pots have been temporarily sunk into a stone trough, which has also been planted with succulents, including echeveria, aeonium and crassula.

mammillaria. Their main attraction is their curious shapes, but they also have spectacular flowers. Found in desert conditions, they must be given the sunniest spot in the house. Although the optimum temperature for many species is 10–15°C (50–60°F), they can tolerate temperatures down to 5°C (41°F), or even lower in winter if the compost is kept dry. A south or west-facing windowsill is the ideal situation, particularly in a cool room where they can rest during winter.

● **forest cacti** originate from tropical forests and grow naturally in the

flowering cacti displays

Some cacti species flower more easily than others, so nurseries often stick dried helichrysum flowers around the crowns of plants that are reluctant to flower, such as echinocactus (above), to make them more saleable. Only the cactus on the left bears true flowers. Among the best flowering desert cacti are echinopsis, mammillarias, parodias and rebutias. A pot-bound cactus flowers more readily than one growing in plenty of compost, so repot only when a plant becomes top-heavy.

Forest cacti, such as Christmas cactus (below), will bloom well if you give them a cool and fairly dry rest period after flowering, and place them outdoors during summer.

Christmas cactus (*Schlumbergera*) flowers best in bright indirect light and moderate humidity. Flower buds may drop if the conditions are too dry, and flowering can be delayed or even suppressed if the plants have too much light.

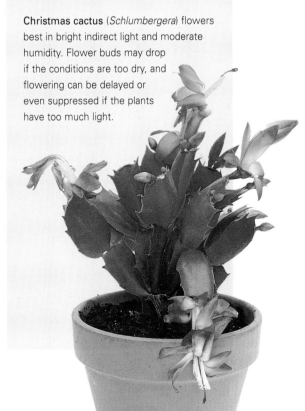

detritus that collects in the nooks and crannies of trees. They include Christmas cactus (*Schlumbergera*) and Easter cactus (*Hatiora rosea*).

Forest cacti, also called epiphytic cacti, need protection from really hot sun in summer and require more regular watering during the growing season than desert cacti. Their dormancy and growth seasons vary considerably depending on the species. While dormant they should be kept at a minimum of 10°C (50°F); in the growing and flowering season, keep them within 13–21°C (55–70°F).

general care

Water cacti and succulents when in active growth, but only when the compost has almost dried out. At the same time, feed them regularly with cactus fertiliser. When dormant, keep the compost for desert cacti dry, and just moist for forest cacti and succulents.

Cacti and succulents are usually sold in clay or plastic pots, in which they can remain for at least two or three years. If repotting, be sure to use pots with holes in the base and a specialised cactus compost, which is gritty, coarse and free draining.

cacti & succulents/2

displaying cacti

Desert cacti look best in a group, either in individual pots or planted together in a wide, shallow bowl or pan to make a cactus garden (see page 140). If you set the individual pots in an outer container, make sure they are never allowed to stand in water.

When planting cacti together in one container include a variety of shapes and types – round, tall and squat ones as well as spiny, furry and hooked cacti. Leave plenty of space between plants to allow for growth, as you do not want to be constantly repotting.

A cactus garden suits a minimalist, uncluttered situation. It will thrive in a hot sunny room or conservatory, and is an excellent alternative to more conventional plants where the daytime temperature is exceptionally high in summer but chilly in winter. For best results, plant your cactus garden between late spring and late summer.

Many forest cacti are pendulous, which makes them ideal for display in a hanging basket (see far right).

displaying succulents

Succulents tend to be more versatile than cacti, fitting in more comfortably with other houseplants and a wider range of interior décor. Their rather sombre foliage can be cheered up by brightly coloured or decorated pots, or with one or two seasonal flowering plants alongside.

Small rosette-forming succulents such as *Echeveria secunda* var. *glauca*, haworthia and orostachys can be combined in a dish, with one or two taller branching species for extra interest. Lithops, too, make a pleasing display if several are planted together in a shallow terracotta pan in a similar way to a cactus garden (see page 140).

Succulents can be successfully grown together in a dish garden with certain cacti, provided all the plants enjoy similar conditions of light, compost, feeding and watering. Otherwise group them in their individual pots, using cacti with a branching or spreading habit, such as rat's tail cactus, cereus and *Heliocereus speciosus*.

combination planting

Succulents mix well visually with most non-succulent foliage houseplants – the drawback being that, in general, they need better light. However, a few, such as money tree (*Crassula ovata*), ox-tongue plant (*Gasteria*) and haworthia, prefer a bright sunless spot, so will grow well alongside aspidistras, three-men-in-a-boat (*Tradescantia spathacea*), figs (*Ficus*), prayer plants (*Maranta*) and peperomias.

The houseplants that can cope with the bright light required by most succulents tend to be those with multicoloured leaves – spider plants (*Chlorophytum comosum*), polka dot plants (*Hypoestes phyllostachya*) and velvet plant (*Gynura aurantiaca*) – and most flowering houseplants. Those in flower during winter and early spring, such as azalea (*Rhododendron simsii*), chrysanthemums, primulas and poinsettias (*Euphorbia*

Group plants with different watering and feeding needs in separate pots within the main tray. This one (left) includes crassulas, echeverias and adromischus. The handles on this metal tray are useful for carrying plants outside for their summer holiday.

Desert cacti such as this echinocactus (right) need well-drained potting compost and good light in order to flourish.

Succulents mix well with 'ordinary' houseplants provided they have similar cultural needs. Here, echeveria, aeonium and red-flowered kalanchoe have been placed with an undemanding spider plant.

pulcherrima) are extremely useful for brightening up a succulent collection.

Some succulent houseplants are also widely used for patio decoration in summer or are plunged in a border, although they must be brought inside for winter. Dark-foliaged *Aeonium arboreum* 'Atropurpureum', *A.* 'Zwartkop', spiky agaves, *Aloe ferox*, money tree and *Echeveria harmsii* are all suitable for this purpose.

cacti and succulents
suitable for hanging pots

Many cacti and succulents are trailing and therefore a natural choice for suspended containers. Forest cacti, in particular, look spectacular in a ceramic or wicker hanging pot, situated in good light but out of direct sunshine, near a north or east-facing window. The string-like stems of some succulents can form a bead-like curtain if several plants are hung by a bright window. Rat's tail cactus (*Aporocactus flagelliformis*) will also cope with sun, but it has sharp spines and should not be positioned where it could scratch anyone.

As with all houseplants in hanging pots, the whole plant should receive an equal amount of light throughout the year, otherwise it will grow lop-sided and the shaded part will soon lose colour and condition. The easiest way to achieve a well-shaped specimen is to attach the hanging basket or pot to a swivel hook, obtainable from most garden centres and hardware stores. Connect the hook to a strong bracket or ceiling hook that has been firmly secured to a wall or ceiling, and give the plant a quarter-turn every day, throughout the year.

FOREST CACTI FOR HANGING POTS
● chain cactus (*Rhipsalis paradoxa*) ● Christmas cactus (*Schlumbergera truncata*)
● Easter cactus (*Hatiora rosea*)
● mistletoe cactus (*Rhipsalis baccifera*)
● rat's tail cactus (*Aporocactus flagelliformis*)

Sedum morganianum 'Baby Burr'

SUCCULENTS FOR HANGING POTS
● *Crassula* 'Hottentot' ● donkey's tail (*Sedum morganianum*) ● rosary vine (*Ceropegia linearis* subsp. *woodii*)
● *Sedum sieboldii* 'mediovariegatum'
● string of beads (*Senecio rowleyanus*)

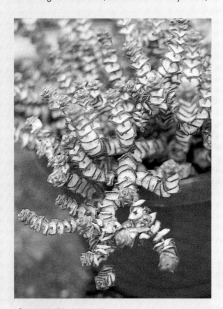

Crassula 'Hottentot'

edible houseplants

An extensive range of vegetables, salads, herbs and fruit can be grown indoors, especially if you have a conservatory. They are fun to grow and conveniently close at hand for checking their needs and development. Pick them young when they are flavoursome and juicy.

indoor vegetables

Conservatories and windowsills are good sites for growing vegetables. Put heavy containers on the floor or a firm support. Some vegetable plants, including trailing species, are suitable for growing in hanging baskets fitted with integral drip trays. Mushrooms are straightforward if you have space in a dark cupboard. Some plants such as chicory and rhubarb can be forced to produce their crop earlier than normal (see page 47).

● **tomatoes, peppers and aubergines**
These easily raised tender crops are favourites for a sunny windowsill and can be grown from seed or small plantlets. For window boxes or hanging baskets, choose pendent varieties such as 'Tumbler' tomatoes. Train cordon varieties such as 'Sweet Million' tomatoes up canes or string in a conservatory, where they will produce long trusses of tasty, decorative tomatoes for several months. Peppers and aubergines are less prolific.

● **carrots and radishes** Most root crops need greater depth than you can provide indoors, but radishes, especially round or globe varieties that do not root very deeply, grow well in boxes, troughs and pans. Seeds can be sown from late winter until mid-autumn, often producing usable roots 21–25 days later. Round carrot varieties are also successful in pots and boxes.

● **potatoes** Seed tubers used for outdoor plantings are easily grown in large pots,

A single tomato plant can produce as much as 5kg (12lb) of fruit, provided it is watered regularly and fed with a tomato fertiliser.

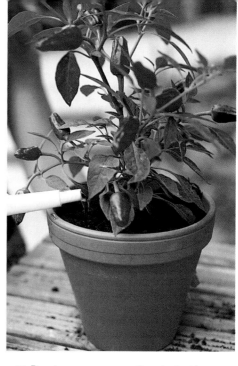

raising chilli peppers on a windowsill

1 Fill a pot with moist seed compost, level the surface and sow seeds thinly, covering them with a sprinkling of compost. Cover with plastic film and stand in good light but not direct sunlight on a windowsill.

2 When the seeds germinate, remove the plastic film, and water carefully to keep the compost just moist. When large enough to handle by the leaves, transplant each seedling into an individual pot and place on a bright windowsill.

3 Repot as necessary until each plant is in a 20cm (8in) pot. Keep the plants in a warm sunny spot. Feed flowering plants every 7–10 days with a tomato fertiliser during the growing season.

buckets or even plastic sacks, and produce worthwhile yields of tasty new potatoes. These are particularly welcome if planted for Christmas use – this should be done in early September with an early variety of potato. When planting the tubers, leave space at the top of the container for adding more compost to earth up the plants as they develop. The top of the sack can be rolled down to start with, then rolled up, as required.

● **mushrooms** Mushrooms are an ideal indoor crop for any time of year. Prepared bags of special compost with mushroom spawn only need watering before being left in a draught-free, dark place such as an attic or cupboard. Keep at 10–15°C (50–60°F) and mushrooms should be cropping a few weeks later. Alternatively make your own compost with straw and a purchased activator. Pack this mixture in a sterile container, such as a large plastic bucket. When the initial heat has died down

and the mixture is turning into compost, add the spawn (which is available in packets).

● **beans and peas** Dwarf french beans can be sown in pots from late winter onwards for early pods. Dwarf broad beans and dwarf runner beans crop well indoors, too. Tall runner beans grown on cane wigwams or on string up the side of a sunny conservatory are decorative as well as productive, and both dwarf and tall mangetout peas will do well as houseplants. Pick the pods while they are young, tender and juicy.

Support beans and peas with twiggy sticks or bamboo canes inserted firmly into the potting compost at the same time as sowing.

Aubergine plants (left) require temperatures of at least 18°C (64°F) and high levels of sunlight and humidity if they are to develop edible fruits such as these.

secrets of success

● dwarf, compact or early varieties of vegetables crop sooner and usually need less space than taller varieties. Those listed in catalogues as 'baby' vegetables are particularly suitable.

● always use fresh seed and potting compost. Garden soil may contain weed seeds as well as pests and disease organisms.

● regular watering is essential for fast uninterrupted growth, which all crops require for top-quality produce. Check plants daily, but avoid over-watering.

● feed with a balanced liquid fertiliser high in nitrogen for leafy crops or high in potash for tomatoes and all fruiting vegetables such as peas, beans and peppers. Apply regularly at the recommended rates.

● gather crops while they are young, otherwise quality deteriorates and plants may stop flowering and fruiting.

edible houseplants/2

salads and herbs

Seedling salads and herbs are among the easiest edible crops to grow indoors.

windowsill salads

For fresh and tasty salads try growing lettuces, rocket (*Eruca vesicaria* subsp. *sativa*), alfalfa, perilla (shiso), oriental leaves such as chopsuey greens, and pots of salad onions.

● **seedling crops** Many salad leaves including mixed lettuces, rocket and chicories can been grown as seedling crops, as can mustard, cress and rape. Sow the seeds thinly in seed trays or pans of potting compost and place on a warm light windowsill, where germination should be rapid. When the seedlings are 8–10cm (3–4in) tall, use scissors to cut off sufficient for immediate use, leaving stumps 1–2.5cm (½–1in) high. These will usually sprout more leaves to give up to three further cuts before plants are exhausted. For continuity, sow a small batch every few weeks.

● **sprouting seeds** Alfalfa and fenugreek seeds can be sprouted in glass jars, either in the dark to blanch the shoots, or in a cool light place to green up (below). Use the seedlings in salads and sandwiches or, in the case of mung bean sprouts, in stir-fries.

● **salad onions and garlic** Grow salad onions in deep trays or pots, either unthinned if the leaves are wanted for flavouring, or spaced out to make small bulbs. It is possible to grow garlic indoors in deep pots, and chives will grow all year round on a windowsill.

● **cucumbers** As cucumbers need humid conditions, they do best in a kitchen or bathroom where they are always warm and can revel in a steam-laden atmosphere. Outdoor, or ridge, varieties are easier to manage than greenhouse types and can be grown in hanging pots or baskets. Grow tall varieties up canes or string for support.

indoor herbs

Herbs are both useful and attractive. Most can be grown in small pots while they are young: either buy small plants, or raise your own from seeds or cuttings. Keep several pots of your favourites, with one for picking on the kitchen windowsill and others in reserve, growing in a spare room or in a sheltered part of the garden.

Perennials such as chives, mint, thyme and rosemary benefit from a respite period out of doors from time to time in spring and summer, otherwise they will grow leggy and can become prone to disease. Stand them in a sunny sheltered place and keep them well watered. In late summer feed with a high-potash fertiliser before bringing them indoors for winter use.

Several plants have edible flowers that can be used to add flavour and eye-catching colour to salads and other culinary dishes. Try growing a few of the following on your windowsill: chives, nasturtium (*Tropaeolum*), pinks (*Dianthus*), pot marigold (*Calendula*), primroses (*Primula vulgaris*) and violets (*Viola odorata*).

STANDARD HERB TIP You can train evergreen herbs such as rosemary, lavender, lemon verbena and myrtle to make a miniature standard tree. Tie a single-stemmed young herb to a cane. Pinch out the growing tip when it reaches the desired height, from where sideshoots will form a bushy head if they are pinched out regularly.

sprouting seeds in a jar

1 Place a teaspoon of alfalfa or fenugreek seeds in a jam jar. To wash off a natural chemical produced by the plant that inhibits premature germination, fill the jar with water almost to the top, screw the top on firmly and shake vigorously for several minutes Strain through muslin and repeat the rinsing twice more.

2 Cover the jar with clean muslin, or similar material, secured with a rubber band, and stand in bright but indirect light. Wash the seeds twice a day, straining off as much water as possible through the muslin to prevent the seeds from turning mouldy. The nutritious seedlings grow rapidly and can be eaten in three or four days. There will be several servings in a 450g (1lb) jar.

Marjoram, rosemary and thyme are herbs of mediterranean origin and will thrive on a sunny windowsill.

kitchen herb pot

Using a special herb pot with holes in the sides is another popular way of growing culinary herbs indoors (right). Choose herbs with a pleasant aroma and include some coloured-leaved varieties such as purple basil (*Ocimum basilicum* var. *purpurascens*) or golden sage (*Salvia officinalis* 'Kew Gold'). Make sure you select herbs that require similar growing conditions. Among the most suitable are sage, thyme, parsley, marjoram, basil and rosemary.

A herb pot will usually last all summer. You can replant it for winter and spring, using young plants that you have grown from cuttings or some that have been purchased.

planting a herb pot

YOU WILL NEED • clay herb pot
• crocks or other drainage material
• herbs of your choice • potting compost

1 **Cover the base of the pot** with crocks, then add compost to just below the first holes. Plant the bottom layer of herbs (here, sage and marjoram), laying each rootball on its side and working its top growth gently out through a hole. Add further layers of compost and herbs until all the holes are filled.

2 **Plant the top** of the herb pot with your chosen herb (here, rosemary). Water thoroughly, then place the pot on a drip tray by a sunny window. When the herbs have established, pinch out the growing tips to encourage bushiness.

edible houseplants/3

growing fruits

If you have a spacious, airy sunroom, conservatory or glazed porch, you can grow a variety of potted fruits, including figs, citrus and grapes. Apricots and peaches often crop earlier and better under cover than outdoors, although they benefit from spending the warm summer months out in the garden, as do most types of fruit trees and shrubs.

With the exception of strawberries, most fruit-producing plants are trees or shrubs that need a deep and nutritious root run, so choose containers that are at least 30cm (12in) in diameter and a little more in depth. As plants grow, move them into larger pots or small tubs. You can also root prune them each year to maintain a convenient size (see page 139). Alternatively, for mature plants, remove just the top 5–10cm (2–4in) of soil in the pot and replace this with fresh compost each spring.

In general use a soil-based compost, such as John Innes No.3, placed over a generous layer of drainage material such as earthenware crocks, pebbles or gravel. Water and feed regularly, especially while plants are bearing flowers and fruit, when a high-potash fertiliser is recommended.

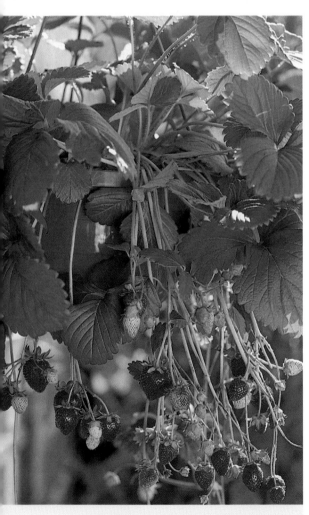

The delicious trailing fruits on alpine strawberries are particularly eye-catching and easy to crop when the plants are grown in a hanging basket. Keep them well watered, and feed both in flower and fruit.

- **peaches and nectarines** Natural or 'genetically' dwarf varieties such as 'Bonanza' (peach) and 'Nectarella' (nectarine) can be grown as short standards on 75cm (30in) stems. Keep them indoors in a well-lit, sunny position in temperatures of 10–13°C (50–55°F) until fruit sets, when they will require higher temperatures of 18–21°C (65–70°F). Ventilate freely in warm weather

- **apricots** Compact varieties such as 'Shipleys' and 'Goldcot' on semi-dwarfing 'St Julien A' rootstocks are highly productive in pots, especially if they are trained against a sunny conservatory wall. For apricots, use a soil-less potting compost (not a soil-based one) over plenty of drainage material. To ensure fruit, hand pollinate by transferring pollen from one flower to another with a paintbrush.

- **mulberry** This slow-growing tree is ideal for a large pot. For tasty fruits that ripen in early summer, grow the black mulberry *Morus nigra* 'Chelsea' in bright, indirect light in a well-ventilated spot, at 13–21°C (55–70°F).

- **cape gooseberries** The cape gooseberry (*Physalis pruinosa*) and

Many dessert varieties of grape crop heavily in a sunny, well-ventilated conservatory or sunroom, but some including the choicest muscat varieties need extra warmth, to 20°C (68°F), in autumn to ripen the fruit well.

ground cherry (*P. angulata*) both make bushy pot plants, with small, tomato-like, white flowers and cherry-size, yellow or red fruits in papery husks. They are very prolific when grown in large pots, 30cm (12in) or more across, in direct sunlight near a window.

- **dwarf pomegranate** For pot cultivation, choose the small *Punica granatum* var. *nana*, which grows only 90cm (3ft) high and often produces its conspicuous scarlet flowers while relatively immature. Attractive miniature fruits follow in early autumn but seldom ripen. Plenty of ventilation and sunlight are needed, especially in late summer and autumn.

- **figs** All varieties fruit more heavily if their roots are confined to a large pot, but 'Negro Largo' does particularly well as a houseplant. A temperature range of 13–18°C (55–65°F) can limit the mature size of the plant, but it may still be necessary to prune in summer and winter to control exuberant growth. Set in a well-lit spot away from direct sun, and feed the plant sparingly two or three times in the growing season.

● **grapes** A vine provides shade and looks ornamental trained up walls and across the roof of a conservatory. Ventilate freely to prevent mildew spoiling the fruit. Each winter, shorten the sideshoots back to two buds.

● **strawberries** Alpine strawberries in pots on a sunny windowsill will fruit almost continuously from early summer until mid-autumn. Large-fruited strawberries will also do well, and are especially valuable when forced to produce early fruit. To stimulate early strawberries, pot up plants in autumn in 13–15cm (5–6in) pots and leave in a well-lit room. The plants should develop edible crops from late spring onwards, after which they can be discarded or planted out in the garden to grow on.

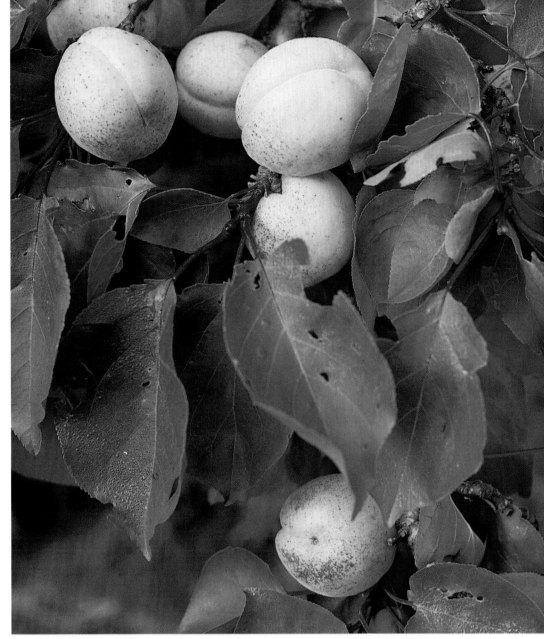

Nectarines and peaches (here, 'Peregrine') have a long showy flowering season during spring. The flowers need to be hand pollinated if they are to develop into delicious fruit.

citrus trees

Citrus plants such as lemons, oranges and kumquats are handsome all year round with evergreen, glossy or leathery leaves, fragrant white flowers, and fruits even on quite small plants. They can be bought as young plants or grown from seed (see page 152). All citrus varieties prefer cool rather than hot conditions and can suffer indoors at temperatures much above 21°C (70°F), unless kept in at least 50 per cent humidity.

● Keep plants evenly moist at all times, and feed during spring and summer with a citrus plant food.

● In early summer, stand plants on a warm, sheltered patio or by an open window, away from scorching sunshine.

● Bring the trees indoors again in early autumn, just prior to the first frosts.

● To maintain an attractive bushy shape, pinch out the tips of new shoots when

they reach the desired length, or carefully trim the whole plant during late winter.

● Give citrus plants good light and a minimum temperature of 5°C (40°F) during winter.

● As they develop, repot young plants in increasingly large containers filled with ericaceous (lime-free) compost. This should be done in spring.

Citrus trees such as this kumquat (Fortunella japonica) bear scented flowers followed by edible fruits.

fun plants

It can be relatively easy to grow a mini pineapple, date palm or lemon tree, or many other exotic plants, from a seed, pip or cutting. It is very rewarding, and you will gain some unusual free houseplants – but in most cases don't expect too much in the way of fruit.

Why not have fun experimenting with some of these plant ideas? Children will also enjoy them, as they are quick to do and can produce quirky results.

sprouting tops and roots

Try growing pieces of carrot top, ginger root or a sweet potato tuber bought from a greengrocer or supermarket. The leafy top cut from a pineapple can also be sprouted into a plant.

● **carrot tops** Cut off the top of a carrot, just below where the leaves grow. Sit it in a shallow saucer of water or push it gently into the surface of a small pot of damp compost. Ferny leaves will soon appear, and eventually small white flower heads too. You can also grow plants from beetroot and parsnip tops.

● **ginger** Fill a seed tray with potting compost and push in a piece of fresh ginger root, or rhizome, placing it so any obvious buds point sideways. Half cover with moist potting compost and set in a warm, humid position. The cutting will soon start to produce shoots and roots. However, for the ginger plant to remain healthy and flower, it needs jungle conditions of high temperature and humidity.

● **sweet potatoes** Buy a sweet potato tuber that is suitable for cooking and bury it in a grow bag or a tub filled with

Sprout sweet potatoes (left) and pineapples (right) in a sunny position in a temperature of 24–30°C (75–86°F). The sweet potato will flourish if grown in potting compost or even in water (as here). For more plants that are suitable for growing in water see page 44.

potting compost. Keep indoors in a warm, well-lit position. The sweet potato will gradually produce shoots and roots. Earth up the shoots as they develop. When the stems start to wilt, dig up the plant and eat the crop of sweet potatoes buried in the compost.

● **pineapples** Purchase a whole fresh pineapple with a healthy, green, medium-sized top from a supermarket or greengrocer. Remove the top of the pineapple along with some of the basal leaves. Put the stump on its side in an airing cupboard or warm greenhouse to dry out, until roots form around the base. It can then be potted up into very well-draining compost such as bromeliad compost. As the plant grows, move it into a larger container and eventually it will produce a baby pineapple from a central shoot.

peanuts

These are great fun to grow as they behave so unexpectedly. Make sure you use shelled raw peanuts; those that have been roasted or salted will not germinate. Push the peanuts into pots

growing a pineapple top

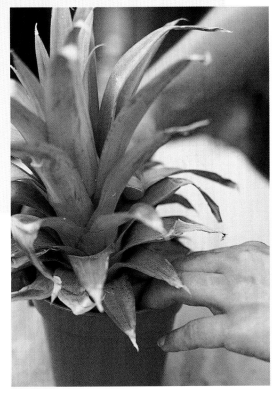

1 Cut off the top of the pineapple using a sharp knife. Strip off the small bottom leaves to reveal a clear stump of about 2.5cm (1in). Leave the stump to dry until roots develop around the base. Rub off any dead tissue and leaves.

2 Push the stump gently into a small pot filled with bromeliad compost. Move the pot into a well-lit position at a temperature of at least 18°C (65°F). New foliage will gradually develop through the top of the pineapple.

of damp seed compost, and they will sprout into tender annual plants with pea-like flowers. As the flowers fade, the stems of the plant bend down into the compost (they may need a little guidance) until the heads are buried. The knobbly pods form underground, hence the alternative name of groundnut.

planting peanuts

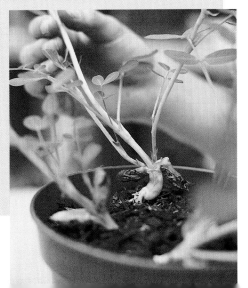

1 Push the unroasted peanuts into small pots of moist seed compost. Place the pots in a warm propagator, or cover them with a sealed polythene bag. Leave in a dark place such as an airing cupboard, while the seeds germinate.

2 Once a seedling emerges, remove the cover and position the pot in a well-lit spot in quite a high humidity of at least 75 per cent (see page 32) and a temperature of 20–30°C (68–86°F). Keep well watered and mist daily to keep up humidity if necessary.

3 When the seedlings are 10–15cm (4–6in) tall, transplant them into a pot 30cm (12in) across. Reduce humidity levels while the plants are flowering, to aid pollination.

fun plants/2

pips and seeds

Seeds from bought vegetables and fruit, such as tomatoes, peppers, aubergines and melons, will germinate easily on a warm, sunny windowsill (see page 145). You can also try growing seeds from apples, citrus and more exotic fruits you have just eaten, or even experiment with growing fresh coffee beans, as long as you make sure they have not been roasted.

The results can often be very interesting, although any fruit produced by your seedling tree will be different to the fruit that enclosed the original pip or stone. The exceptions are peaches and nectarines, which can produce crops of typical, well-flavoured fruit on a tree grown from a stone and trained against a sunny wall. Seed-raised grape seedlings seldom produce satisfactory crops but are worth growing for the foliage alone (see page 148).

temperate fruit trees

Apple, pear, plum, cherry or peach trees can be grown from seed.
● Pop two or three stones or pips into a small pot filled with seed or multipurpose potting compost. Place the pot, sealed in a polythene bag, in the refrigerator for a few weeks – this will speed up germination – then bring it out into a cool light spot indoors. The pips or stones will germinate if the compost is kept moist, though this may take months in the case of a stone.
● Once the seedlings are big enough to handle by the leaves, separate them and pot them on individually into successively larger pots. Use John Innes No.1 compost for the first two

Peat pellets can be used to germinate individual seeds. Saturate the pellets in water, then insert a seed. Keep the pellet slightly moist while the seed germinates.

moves, then John Innes No.2 and finally No.3 when they need a 45cm (18in) pot. At this stage they can be kept without further potting on, for many years if regularly watered and fed throughout the growing season with a liquid high-potash fertiliser. Alternatively transplant your young tree into open ground in the garden, where it can grow even larger.

citrus trees

Some of the prettiest plants can be raised from citrus pips – oranges, lemons, grapefruit, clementines. The pips germinate easily at any time, but make the best plants if sown in spring and early summer. Germination times vary but two or three seedlings should have appeared in a month or so. Feed in spring and summer with a citrus plant food.

Eventually citrus plants form bushy shrubs and will produce edible fruit, but it may taste very sour. If the plants become large, prune them to a manageable size, although this will affect fruit production (see page 149).

tropical trees

A few exotic seeds such as coffee, dates and avocado develop into interesting indoor plants.
● **dates** Small date (*Phoenix dactylifera*) seedlings can develop if date stones are simply pushed into the compost of a houseplant during the

growing a lemon tree

1 Insert about six lemon pips in a small pot of seed compost, spaced evenly and about 1cm (½in) deep. Water well. Put in a propagator or cover with the bottom of a clear plastic bottle.

2 When the seedlings are big enough to handle, separate them carefully. Then transplant them into individual small pots filled with ericaceous (lime-free) compost.

3 Set the potted plants in cool conditions in bright, but indirect light (see page 149). As the plants increase in size, move them into larger pots. Pinch prune them to create a bushy shape, or trim the whole plant to size during late winter.

This coffee plant (*Coffea arabica*) was grown from an unroasted bean sown in spring. Flowering and fruiting may occur after three or four years.

date palm

1 **Soak date stones** in water for 48 hours. Plant them vertically in a pot filled with compost. Place in a propagator or cover the pot with a sealed polythene bag and set in an airing cupboard.

2 **As soon as the seeds** show signs of growth, uncover them and move the pots into good light. When 8–10cm (3–4in) tall, plant in individual pots and grow on as for phoenix palms (see page 101).

Christmas festivities. If a young palm germinates in this way, remove it together with the remains of the date stone, and pot it up in potting compost. It should produce a pleasing specimen plant for several years, although it will eventually grow too large for the home. To grow a date palm in a more conventional way, see above.

● avocado pears Remove the stone from the fruit, and cut 1cm (½in) off the pointed tip. Push the stone into moist compost with the cut tip just showing. The resulting tree grows tall and looks rather like a rubber plant. To encourage branching and a bushier shape, pinch out the growing tip. If grown in a heated conservatory, an avocado plant may mature fully and produce fruit. You can grow lychees in a similar way.

index

acknowledgments

Photographs were supplied by the following people and organisations. Abbreviations are used as follows: **t** top, **c** centre, **b** bottom, **l** left, **r** right. **F&PA** Flowers & Plants Association, **RD** Reader's Digest copyright **LE** Liz Eddison, **JH** John Hanby, **GPL** Garden Picture Library, **HR** Howard Rice, **FS** Friedrich Strauss, **MW** Mark Winwood

Front cover RD/MW **Back cover** all RD/MW **01** GPL/M O'Hara **02-03** GPL/FS **04-05** RD/MW **06-07** all RD/MW **08-09** RD/MW **10** tl GPL/L Burgess, tr M. O'Hara, bl GPL/FS **11** tl LE, tr GPL/ A. Lord, br GPL/FS, bl GPL/HR **12** l GPL/FS, tr F&PA, br GPL/FS **13** tl GPL/L Burgess, tr GPL/FS, br GPL/M O'Hara, bl LE **14** tl RD/MW, r F&PA, bl GPL/FS **15** tl LE, tr GPL/ L Brotchie, br F&PA, bl F&PA **16** l GPL/HR, tr GPL/FS, br LE **17** tl F&PA, tc GPL/L Brotchie, tr GPL/C Rosenfeld, br LE, bl F&PA **18** l F&PA, tr F&PA, br GPL/FS **19** tl F&PA, tc F&PA, tr F&PA, br LE, bl F&PA **20** tl M O'Hara, r M O'Hara, bl F&PA **21** tl M O'Hara, tc RD/MW, tr RD/MW, br LE, bl F&PA **22-23** RD/MW **24-25** RD/MW **26** bl RD/MW, tr GPL/FS **27** tl F&PA, tc M O'Hara, all on r RD/MW **28** RD/MW **29** all RD/MW except t F&PA **30** RD/MW **31** l RD/MW, r GPL/FS **32-33** RD/MW **34-35** RD/MW **36-37** RD/MW **38-39** RD/MW **40-41** RD/MW **42-43** RD/MW **44-45** RD/MW **46** GPL/MLS **47** all RD/MW except t LE **48-49** RD/MW **50-51** RD/MW **52-53** RD/MW **54-55** RD/MW **56-57** RD/MW **58-59** RD/MW **60-61** RD/MW **62-63** RD/MW **64-65** RD/MW **66-67** RD/MW **68-69** RD/MW **70-71** RD/MW **72-73** RD/MW **74-75** RD/MW **76** RD/MW **77** all RD/MW except br GPL/FS **78-79** RD/MW **80-81** RD/MW **82-83** RD/MW **84** RD/MW **85** t GPL/N Holmes, br RD/MW **86-87** RD/MW **88-89** RD/MW **90-91** RD/MW **92-93** RD/MW **94-95** RD/MW **96-97** RD/MW **98-99** RD/MW **100-101** RD/MW **102** l RD/MW r GPL/FS **103** RD/MW **104-105** RD/MW **106-107** RD/MW **108-109** RD/MW **110-111** RD/MW **112-113** RD/MW **114-115** RD/MW **116-117** RD/MW **118-119** F&PA **120-121** RD/MW **122-123** RD/MW **124** t F&PA, b F&PA **125** tl Oka, tr RD/MW, cr LE, c GPL/P. Bergdahl, cl F&PA **126-127** RD/MW **128-129** RD/MW **130** RD/MW **131** t F&PA, b RD/MW **132-133** RD/MW **134** RD/MW **135** all RD/MW except br LE **136** bl Stowasis, tr GPL/R Sutherland **137** RD/MW **138** cl RD/MW b JH **139** all JH except tl RD/MW, tr RD/MW **140-141** RD/MW **142-143** RD/MW **144** GPL/M Howes **145** all RD/MW except t GPL/D Askham **146** RD/MW **147** all RD/MW except t LE **148** l GPL/FS, tr MT **149** tr GPL/Lamontagne, b RD/MW **150-151** RD/MW **152-153** RD/MW **back cover** RD/MW

Front cover: *Clivia miniata* **Back cover** clockwise from top left: pinching out african violet, *Aucuba japonica* 'Crotonifolia', *Sinningia speciosa* hybrid, propagating a plantlet, *Dionaea muscipula*, *Solenostemon scutellarioides* hybrid

Amazon Publishing would like to thank Adrian Hall Garden Centres for allowing the practical photography to be done at their Feltham nursery. Many thanks to Kate Kenyan and Veronica Richardson of The Flowers & Plants Association, John Hanby for his help with Indoor Bonsai, Lucinda Lachelin at RHS Wisley for advice on orchids, Oka for the picture on page 125 and Stowasis Garden Centre for their picture on page 136. Thanks also to Penny Boylan for decorating the pots on pages 120-123.

Reader's Digest would like to thank The Van Hage Garden Company of Ware, Hertfordshire, for allowing us to use their premises and providing the plants for most of the photography in the Plant Selector.

Year-round Indoor Gardening is part of a series of gardening books called the **All-Season Guide to Gardening**. It was created for Reader's Digest by Amazon Publishing Limited.

Editors Joanna Chisholm, Barbara Haynes, Jackie Matthews
Design Maggie Aldred, Karen Stewart, Alison Tumer
Writers Andi Clevely, Daphne Ledward, Anne Swithinbank, Sarah Wilson
Photographic direction Gillian Shaw
Consultant Sarah Wilson
Editorial Assistant Lucy Doncaster
Indexer Hilary Bird

FOR READER'S DIGEST
Project Editor Christine Noble
Project Art Editor Kate Harris
Pre-press Accounts Manager Penny Grose

READER'S DIGEST GENERAL BOOKS
Editorial Director Cortina Butler
Art Director Nick Clark

We are committed to both the quality of our products and the service we provide to our customers. We value your comments, so please feel free to contact us on **08705 113366**, or via our website at **www.readersdigest.co.uk**
If you have any comments about the content of our books, you can email us at gbeditorial@readersdigest.co.uk

Origination Colour Systems Limited, London
Printed and bound in Europe by Arvato Iberia

ISBN 0 276 42878 1
BOOK CODE 621-008-01
CONCEPT CODE UK0087